Key Stage 3

D1632926

English

Ages 12–13

ALSAGER LIBRARY
FOR REFERENCE ONLY
NOT TO BE TAKEN AWAY

PLEASE RENEW BY

CHESHIRE LIBRARIES	
H J	24/09/2001
428	£4.99
GT	

Lynn Huggins Cooper

survival GUIDE

Acknowledgements

The author and publisher are grateful to the copyright holders, as credited, for permission to use quoted materials and photographs.

I is for India by Prodeepta Das, published by Frances Lincoln Ltd, © Prodeepta Das 1996. Reproduced by permission of Frances Lincoln Ltd., 4 Torriano Mews, Torriano Avenue, London NW5 2RZ.
Immortal by Christopher Golden and Nancy Holder, published by Simon & Schuster UK Limited. ™ and © 1999 by Twentieth Century Fox Film Corporation. All Rights Reserved.
Traveller's Child by Jacqueline Brown, published by Oxford University Press. Reproduced by permission of Jacqueline Brown.
I am David by Ann Holm, English translation © 1965 Egmont Books Limited and used with permission.
Caught on the hop... article, reproduced courtesy of Newcastle Chronicle and Journal Ltd.
The West Pier by Dave Huggins, reproduced by permission of the author. Accompanying photographs also by permission of Dave Huggins.
Building the pier by Dr Fred Gray © Brighton West Pier Trust.
The Amber Spyglass by Philip Pullman. Reproduced by permission of AP Watt Ltd on behalf of Philip Pullman.

Every effort has been made to trace the copyright holders and to obtain their permission for the use of copyright material. The author and publisher will gladly receive information enabling them to rectify any error or omission in subsequent editions.

Letts Educational
Chiswick Centre
414 Chiswick High Road
London W4 5TF
Tel: 020 8996 3333
Fax: 020 8996 8390
Email: *mail@lettsed.co.uk*
Website: *www.letts-education.com*

First published 2001

Text © Lynn Huggins Cooper 2001

All our Rights Reserved. No part of this publication may be produced, stored in a retrieval system, or transmitted, in any form or by any means, electronic, mechanical, photocopying, recording or otherwise, without the prior permission of Letts Educational.

British Library Cataloging in Publication Data. A CIP record of this book is available from the British Library.

ISBN 1 84085 634 3

Letts Educational Limited is a division of Granada Learning Limited, part of the Granada Media Group.

Edited and typeset by Cambridge Publishing Management
Designed by Moondisks Limited

English
Book 2 Ages 12-13

Introduction 5

Each unit in this book is targeted at one of the following areas of the Key Stage 3 Literacy Framework: Word level (W), Sentence level (S), Text level – Reading (TR) or Text level – Writing (TW)

Introduction

This book has been written to help you to understand your English classes at school. You have survived your first year at secondary school, and your KS3 Tests are still a year away in Year 9. But students in Year 8 cannot afford to sit back and relax as there are Optional Tests in Year 8 too! This book will help you to prepare for these tests, but it should not be seen as just another exam crammer. English is learned as a process, building progress on the work you have done before. When you sit your KS3 SATs, you are tested on the skills that have you have gained over the course of your time at school – not just what you have learned in Y9!

This book covers many of the areas that you will cover at school during your English lessons. It is written in an easily understandable and (hopefully!) fun way. It should be used to support the work you do at school, and if there is anything you do not understand you should ask your teacher – they should be glad to help and pleased that you have asked. Never be afraid to say to your teacher that you do not understand something, or are finding work difficult; teaching you is the job they have chosen!

The pages of this book are laid out with the things you need to know at the top of the page, and exercises to help you practise at the bottom. The Red Alert feature at the foot of the page usefully reminds you of vital points to remember, and Tactics boards help you to revise the points you have learned. The Jargon Buster facility at the back of the book will help you to understand the technical terms that you will meet during English lessons.

Above all, remember to pace yourself as you use this book, dipping in to it as you need to rather than trying to doggedly work from cover to cover. It is supposed to be a survival guide to make your life easier, not just another book to get stressed about and add to your already heavy workload. Remember to take time to have fun too – how can you write great, imaginative stories, poems and articles if you never have time to experience the great, wide, thrilling world out there? Have fun!

Apostrophes

Apostrophes are used in writing for two purposes:
- to show possession – that something belongs to someone or something;
- to show contraction – that a letter or letters have been dropped from a word.

Examples

The baby's face was smeared with chocolate. (possession)

Examples

"That's my chocolate!" said her brother. (contraction)

Possessive apostrophes

It is easy to show that something belongs to someone or something – simply add an apostrophe + s.

Examples

The whiskers of the cat → The cat's whiskers
The CD of the boy → The boy's CD
The temper of the teacher → The teacher's temper

Exercise 1

Copy out the passages. Add the possessive apostrophes. The first one has been done for you.

1   The tiger's tail swished angrily. She ate her pieces of meat warily, her eyes flicking at every movement. The boy tried not to move, but the insects were biting. Sunil's leg twitched suddenly, and the tiger's eyes found him there.

2   The dogs breath was rancid. The girls nose wrinkled in her sleep, then one eye wearily opened. The girls eyes popped open in surprise as she saw the large shaggy creature bending over her. "Bramble!" she cried. "What are you doing in here? Fetch my slippers, girl!" As she sat up, Beth wondered where the other dogs were.

3   The singers voice was low and mellow, but her eyes were glittering with excitement.

4   The old womans bags were heavy and it was a long way to the bus stop.

5   The magicians wand seemed to have a life of its own. The wands tip sparked and flamed wildly until the performers hat was set alight.

Remember – *it's* only has an apostrophe for the shortened version of *it is* and never when it shows possession (*The cat licked its paw*).

It gets confusing where possessive apostrophes occur when the example already ends in s. When this happens, the apostrophe is sometimes added without the extra s. This is fine, but adding an apostrophe + s is seen as 'correct'.

However, when the word ending in s is a group of people, the apostrophe is added on its own.

Contractions

Examples

The coat of James → James's coat

Examples

The noise of the fans → The fans' noise
The houses of our neighbours →
    The neighbours' houses

I keep feeling that something's missing...

Contractions are words with missing letters. They are usually used in informal writing or in speech.

Common contractions:

I am → I'm	does not → doesn't
I have → I've	I had → I'd
we are → we're	I would → I'd
do not → don't	they are → they're
he will → he'll	shall not → shan't
she will → she'll	will not → won't
who is → who's	you have → you've

Exercise 2

Change the words in these sentences. Write the contractions.
         wasn't   didn't
1 There ~~was not~~ time to go to the shops, so I ~~did not~~ get any milk.
2 The band was not very good. I have seen better.
3 We are not going to the pictures tonight because we have seen the film already.
4 They are not coming to see us, so it does not matter if you can not come.

Exercise 3

Read this passage. Rewrite it without the contractions.
   "It's funny," Bethany said to Sarah. "I don't usually like sporty types, but there's something about him that's attractive."
   "I wouldn't mind a date with him either!" said Sarah.
   "Come on," Bethany sighed. "We've got double maths next, and old Clarkie will go nuts if we're late! And he'll not accept 'Sorry, we were busy eyeing boys' as an excuse!"

RED ALERT RED ALERT RED ALERT RED

Prefixes and suffixes

Understanding the jargon

A prefix is a syllable or set of syllables added to the beginning of a word.
A suffix a syllable or set of syllables added to the end of a word.

You can work out the meanings of many really long and complicated words if you learn the meanings of prefixes and suffixes. When you say things like *mega*, *hyper* and *anti* to your friends, you are really using prefixes. It is acceptable to use these terms in informal settings but not in formal language (see page 16).

Exercise 1

Use your knowledge of prefixes and suffixes to work out the meanings of these words. First break the words down into parts that you recognise.

1   intergalactic – *inter* means *between* and *galactic* means to do with *galaxies*

2   disproportionate

3   extinguish

4   monosyllabic

5   tripartite

6   biography

7   intermediate

8   meaningless

Splitting words up will help you to work out their meanings. Keep a log of new words by listing them under the correct prefix or suffix. **AL**

Read this list of prefixes and suffixes and their meanings.

Prefixes:

anti-	means *against*	dis-	means *not*
auto-	means *self*	inter-	means *between* or *among*
bi-	means *two*	mono-	means *one* or *single*
tri-	means *three*	poly-	means *many*
bio-	means *life*	pre-	means *before*
ex-	means *out of*	ante-	means *before*
in-	means *not*		

Suffixes:

-able   means *able*

-ible   means *able*

-less   added to a word changes its meaning to the opposite (so *fear* + *less* means brave)

It is permissible that the perishable groceries are binned.

It can help to identify the definitions of new words if you learn the meanings of the prefixes and suffixes above – many mysterious and seemingly incomprehensible words will then become clear!

Exercise 2

Read the passage below. Can you identify any prefixes and suffixes?

The students were disinterested in the lecture because the teacher spoke in a monologue. Her voice was boring, but also inaudible. She was completely hopeless, and Rosie automatically slumped back in her seat as the lecture began. Disinterested students fidgeted, sharpened pencils and stared out of windows as the lecturer began to read from her own biography.

The students were <u>dis</u>interest<u>ed</u> …

Ideas and opinions

Understanding the jargon

Paraphrasing is when you put into other words or restate something in your own words.

When you are writing an English essay about a book, a poem or a play, the teacher or examiner is interested in your ideas and opinions. However, you must remember to give evidence to show why you feel as you do. Try to get into the habit of giving a reason for every point that you make, and write answers as though the teacher has not read the text. Explain your reasons in your own words – if you simply copy the extract it does not show your understanding – although you can refer to actual words or phrases that support your point of view. Show when you have used a quotation by surrounding the word or phrase in 'quotation marks'.

Lindsey trudged listlessly out into the garden, her shoulders sagging. She stared at the ground as she walked, not seeing the tapestry of colour that surrounded her. She slumped onto the bench, ignoring the fat

tabby cat that sprang onto her knee. She felt terrible.

Exercise 1

Read this passage and answer the question.

> She slumped onto the bench, ignoring the fat tabby cat that sprang onto her knee. She felt terrible.
> Suddenly, Lindsey heard a noise coming from the hedge. She looked up and saw a freckled face thrust out of the foliage. "James!" she cried in surprise. "I thought you had gone! My dad said you were leaving this morning. What are you doing here?" Her face was flushed, and her eyes shone brightly.

How do Lindsey's feelings change, and why?

We know Lindsey feels depressed . . .

RED Always explain in your own words and remember to paraphrase! If you use the words directly from the text, use quotation marks. **A L**

How did Lindsey feel as she walked into the garden? Here are two possible answers:

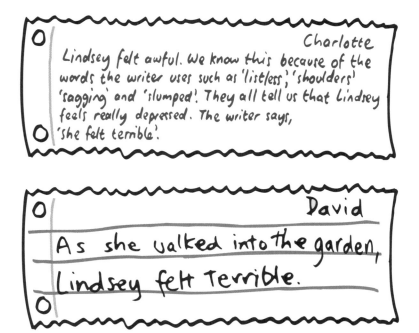

Charlotte

Lindsey felt awful. We know this because of the words the writer uses such as 'listless', 'shoulders' 'sagging' and 'slumped'. They all tell us that Lindsey feels really depressed. The writer says, 'she felt terrible'.

David

As she walked into the garden, Lindsey felt Terrible.

Charlotte's answer would get a good mark. She has given her opinion, in her own words, and backed it up with quotations. David's answer is correct, but he has not shown that he understands what he has read. He has simply copied words directly from the text and has not put his answer in his own words. Copying words is not the same as using quotations and it will actually lose you marks.

So remember:
- Answer questions in your own words
- Give reasons for your opinions
- Use quotations
- Explain the answer as though the teacher has not read the book

Exercise 2

Read the passage below, then paraphrase it. Make sure you cover all the points made in the original passage.

The newts scattered as her shadow fell on the water. Peering out from behind their leaf shelters, they regarded her with the inquisitive faces of tiny brown dragons. Vicky had always found newts fascinating; she thought they looked alien somehow with their fiery orange crests and bright yellow eyes. She remembered collecting newts with her teacher as a special environmental project. Their pond had been drying up, and her class had helped to rehome them in the school pond. She remembered that they had needed special permission to touch the newts as they are a protected species.

The newts swam away when they saw the girl's shadow ...

Speech marks

Talking is easy but writing about talking can be more difficult. There are certain rules about using speech marks, and if you learn them things become much clearer!

Use speech marks before and after the words that are spoken, but not when you are writing about what someone has said.

Example

"My favourite snack is a double-decker cheese and syrup sandwich," said Tina.

Tina said that her favourite snack was a double-decker cheese and syrup sandwich.

Always start words inside speech marks with a capital letter, even when they are not at the beginning of the sentence.

Example

She sighed and said, "I can't wait until lunch time!"

Exercise 1

Copy and correct these sentences by adding speech marks, where appropriate. The first one has been done for you.

1 My mum said that she didn't want to go to Birmingham, but I jumped up and said "I do!"

2 Good grief! said Helen. I'd hate it if I had to live here!

3 Sheila said that she liked living in Brighton because it was at the seaside.

4 It's Hove, actually, Dave complained.

5 I like going on the Pier best, drooled Bethany, because I love the hot doughnut stalls.

6 Alex argued with his sister. He said that he preferred the rock shops under the promenade.

7 Well, I like playing on the beach best! shrieked Eleanor, as she splashed the water at them both.

12

RED Use speech marks around that are actually spoken (direct speech), but not when you are writing about what someone has said (reported speech).

Always end speech with a punctuation mark, inside the speech marks. If the sentence ends at the end of the speech, use a full stop.

David said, "I love this seafood salad."

If the speech is said in surprise, exclamation or is shouted, use an exclamation mark.

"That is disgusting!" exclaimed Alexander.

If the speech is a question, use a question mark.

"Is that a salad or a rockpool?" whispered Meera.

If the sentence continues after the speech, put a comma before the closing speech marks and carry on with the sentence using a lower case letter.

"I don't think I could eat that," said Shaun as he wrinkled his nose.

Exercise 2

| "I love sherbet!" squealed Kevin. | Kevin said that he loved sherbet. |

Read this passage. Rewrite it by removing all the direct speech (shown by the use of speech marks).

"What's the time, Mum?" asked Alexander. "I'm meeting Simon at six."
"Do you need to have your dinner first? It's not ready yet," replied his mother.
"No, I'll reheat it when I get home. I won't be late!"
"Where are you going tonight?" asked his mother.
"Nowhere special," said Alex.
"Nowhere special with or without your entourage?" his mother said with a smile.
"I don't know what you mean!" laughed Alexander.
"I mean the usual troupe of adoring girls that follow you both around!"
"Yeah, right ... whatever ... see you later!"

RED ALERT RED ALERT RED ALERT RED

Special vocabulary

Have you noticed how some subjects at school have their own special vocabulary? Sometimes words used in everyday life are used in school subjects and they mean something totally different – it sometimes feels as though people are just trying to confuse you!

Maths is a prime example. Look, there's that word *prime*! When I used it then, I meant good. But to my maths teacher, it means a number that can only be divided exactly by itself and one. Confusing, isn't it? One of the subjects that seems to have a whole new language in particular is ICT: email, megabytes, floppy disk, hard drive ... it's like learning a foreign language!

Look at the words on the notes below. Victor has dropped the pages and mixed up the meanings. He's matched the first word to the correct meaning, but can you help him with the rest?

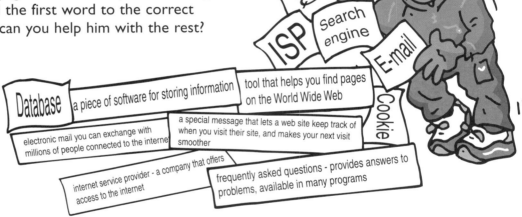

FAQ

ISP

Search engine

E-mail

Cookie

Database | a piece of software for storing information

tool that helps you find pages on the World Wide Web

electronic mail you can exchange with millions of people connected to the internet

a special message that lets a web site keep track of when you visit their site, and makes your next visit smoother

internet service provider - a company that offers access to the internet

frequently asked questions - provides answers to problems, available in many programs

Exercise 1

Translate the following.

1   W84ME – wait for me

2   YRUL8

3   URGR8

4   RUOK

5   OIC

6   BCNU

7   T2UL

8   NO1M8

W84ME YRUL8
URGR8
RUOK   OIC
BCNU
T2UL   NO1M8

There are other forms of special vocabulary. Teenagers have always used code so that their parents can't understand them! Today, many people use 'textspeak', a language made up of abbreviations and numbers, to get messages to their friends quickly using their mobile phone.

> **Examples**
>
> YYUR, YYUB, ICUR, YY4ME *

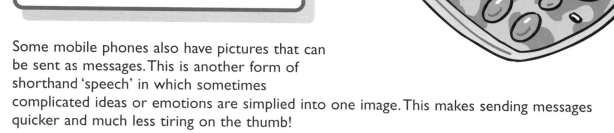

Some mobile phones also have pictures that can be sent as messages. This is another form of shorthand 'speech' in which sometimes complicated ideas or emotions are simplied into one image. This makes sending messages quicker and much less tiring on the thumb!

Look at these pictures. Do you know what each one means?

* Too wise you are, too wise you be, I see you are too wise for me!

Exercise 2

Change these words to short messages using letters and numbers.

1 See you later.   CUL8R
2 Tea for you?
3 Wait for me.
4 You are late.
5 You are a great mate!
6 I see.
7 Be seeing you
8 Thank you

Formal and informal writing

There are two very different styles of writing: formal and informal. Formal writing is the language used in official letters, and is very 'correct'. Informal writing is the 'chatty' style used when you write letters to friends.

This is a formal letter.

12, The Green,
Hampton Forest,
Grundwich GR2 9LR

5 March

Dear Sir/Madam

I am writing to complain about the visit my family made to your establishment on Tuesday 3rd March.

We booked a table for 8pm, which I personally confirmed on the morning of the date in question. When my family and I arrived at your restaurant, we were informed that no table had been reserved for us, and there were none available until 10pm except for a small table adjacent to the bathroom facilities. Since this meal was intended as a birthday treat for my daughter, this news came as a great disappointment. Your staff were kind, but the fact remains that a special evening was somewhat spoiled.

I shall be informing my friends and colleagues with regard to the shoddy service we received.

Yours faithfully

Mrs. Nelson

Exercise 1

You have won a competition, and the prize was to appear on *Celebrity Chompfest* – a programme that pits guest stars against one another in eating contests. You took part, won, and had a party afterwards. You were taken home in a stretch limousine and all the neighbours saw you.

Use the information on these pages to write:
*   A letter to a friend describing your day out.
*   A letter to thank the television company for their hospitality.

Don't forget to think carefully about the audience for your letters. Make sure you choose and use formal or informal terms, as appropriate.

This is an informal letter.

> Hi Harvey!
>
> How are you? Got over the other night yet? I thought my mum was going to pop when that guy said there wasn't a table! I haven't seen her go that ballistic since Lindsey borrowed her leather jacket without asking and then lost it in town! Oh well – all's well that ends well, as my granny says. The restaurant rang this morning and we're getting a meal on the house at the weekend to make up for my 'disappointing experience'. Can you come?
>
> See you later
>
> Judith

Read through both letters, noting any differences you can find in language and style. How can you tell which letter is formal and which is informal? Think about:
- the language
- the phrasing
- the opening and closing phrases . . .

Exercise 2

Which of these words and phrases are 'formal' and which are 'informal'?

require – formal	want – informal
okay	adequate
as soon as you can	at your earliest convenience
won't	will not
excellent	great
inform	tell
ask	enquire
yours sincerely	see you later
suggest	tell

Tactics

Formal language is used for:
- Official letters
- Writing essays
- Notices

Informal language is used for:
- Letters to friends
- Notes
- Diaries

RED ALERT RED ALERT RED ALERT RE

Standard and dialectal language

This message was heard on a telephone line in Newcastle upon Tyne: *Reet Hinny! Are ye gannin doon the toon the neet?*

And this message was heard on a similar line in Sussex: *Right, darling! Are you going into town this evening?*

Which person is speaking 'correctly'? It depends what is meant by 'correct', of course! The two speakers are both talking to friends, so they do not need to use formal speech. What makes their use of language different is dialect – the speaker from Newcastle is using 'Geordie' dialect. Dialectal speech uses different vocabulary and forms of words from standard English and different parts of the country use different dialects.

Dialectal speech is not commonly used when writing, unless a character is speaking in the course of a story, for example. Poetry is sometimes written using dialectal variations of English.

Exercise 1

Think about the way that people speak in your area. Can you think of any words or phrases that only occur locally?

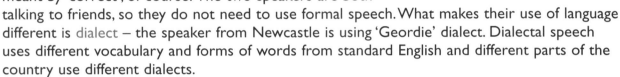

Exercise 2

Read the example of dialectal poetry below.

puddock → frog

> *A puddock sat by the lochan's brim,*
> *An' he thocht there was never a puddock like him.*
> *He sat on his hurdies, he waggled his legs,*
> *An' cockit his heid as he glowered throu' the seggs.*
> From 'The Puddock' by J M Caie

Write out the dialectal words in this poem. What do you think they mean?

18

RED ALERT   Always use the appropriate level of formality for your piece of work.   **A L**

Puns (plays on words) are sometimes made up using dialectal speech to good effect.

Example

Q: What's the difference between David Beckham and Walt Disney?

A: David Beckham plays football and Walt Disney! (*Disnae* is a Scottish dialectal word meaning *doesn't*.)

If we talk using 'standard English', it can sound as though we are being terribly correct.

Read this passage out loud.

Did you use a 'posh' accent?

Don't be fooled – accent and dialect are not the same thing!

The concert was wonderful. I thoroughly enjoyed dancing at the front, and would love another opportunity to see such a spectacle once again.

Accent refers to the way you pronounce words – that is, do you say 'bath' or 'barth' when you describe the place you go to wash?

Now read the non-standard version out loud.

Bet you didn't use such a posh accent for this sentence!

The gig was mega! I had a great time in the moshpit, and can't wait to go again.

Exercise 3

Match the dialectal sentences with their standard English equivalent.

Geordie English	**Standard English**
Ye knaa what ah mean leik.	Please, mother, don't embarrass me.
How man mutha man.	Be careful or we will crash into something.
Eeeh man, ahm gannin te the booza.	Okay, I have had enough, I am going to the bar.
Hoy yer hamma ower heor hinny.	Do you know what I mean?
Whees i' the netty?	Who's in the lavatory?
Gan canny or we'll dunsh summick.	Pass me the hammer darling.

You may like try the dialectal translator on the website whoohoo.co.uk. You can translate phrases into a variety of dialects such as 'Geordie', 'Scouse' and 'Brummie' – and also odd 'dialects' such as 'Yorkshire chicken run' and 'Ali G'!

Modern and old English

Whoever said Shakespeare was boring didn't understand him! Shakespeare's plays were not written for intellectual people – they were written to be acted in front of ordinary people. The plays are like popular action films today, featuring fights, murders, romance, ghosts, witches, epic battles, betrayal, comedy and monstrous villains.

People find Shakespeare's plays hard to understand and, therefore, boring because they are written in the English of his time (late-sixteenth and early-seventeenth century). Many words that were commonly used then have now disappeared. When did you last hear someone pepper their speech with *thee*, *thou*, *methinks* or *prithee*?

Exercise 1

Read this famous passage from the play *Macbeth*.

Macbeth:	Is this a dagger which I see before me,
	The handle toward my hand? Come, let me clutch thee:
	I have thee not, and yet I see thee still.*
	Art thou not, fatal vision, sensible†
	To feeling as to sight? Or art thou but
	A dagger of the mind, a false creation,*
	Proceeding from the heat – oppressed brain?

* I can't get hold of you, but I can still see you.

† Why can't I touch you as well as see you?

* Am I imagining you, because I have a fever?

Now read the following passage from *The Tempest* and explain the underlined words.
(On seeing her future husband, Ferdinand, for the first time, Miranda thinks he is *a spirit*.
Prospero is Miranda's father.)

20

Watch Shakespeare's plays when you can, whether films, at the theatre L or modern versions, to make his writing easier to understand.

The good thing is that to enjoy the plays, and to answer questions on them, you do not have to understand every single word. It is more important that you understand what is going on. In the first instance, it would be a good idea to read the play you are studying in a modernised version. *Shakespeare Stories* and *Shakespeare Stories II* by Leon Garfield (published by Victor Gollancz) are excellent books that keep to the mood of the original plays but are easy to understand as they are written in modern English.

It is also helpful to watch film versions of Shakespeare's plays and the *Animated Tales* series, as well as going to the theatre to see the plays 'live'.

Shakespeare's plays are also difficult to understand at times because they are written in verse or poetry. He also tends to use many words where fewer would, perhaps, be easier to understand!

Exercise 1 continued

> Prospero: *No, <u>wench</u>; it eats and sleeps, and <u>hath</u> such senses*
> *As we have, such: This <u>gallant</u>, which thou seest,*
> *Was in the wreck: and but he's something <u>stain'd</u>*
> *<u>With grief</u>, that's <u>beauty's canker</u>, thou <u>might'st</u>*
> *call him*
> *A goodly person: he hath lost his fellows,*
> *And strays about to find them.*

1	wench – girl	4	stain'd/With grief
2	hath	5	beauty's canker
3	gallant	6	might'st

Exercise 2

Read a speech from one of Shakespeare's plays and 'translate' it into modern English.

> How now wit! whither wander you?
> How are you? Where are you going?

The writing process – fiction

Understanding the jargon

Brainstorming means writing down all your ideas on a subject.

Being given a blank page and told to write a piece of fiction about something such as *The House* is liable to turn adult men and women into gibbering wrecks – yet students are asked to do things like this every day! Instead of staring blankly into space, or panicking, use the following pages to help you to plan a piece of writing to be proud of.

Exercise 1

Write your own brainstorm for a piece of fictional writing called *Alone*.
The story can be of any genre: horror, suspense, adventure, science fiction, romance ...

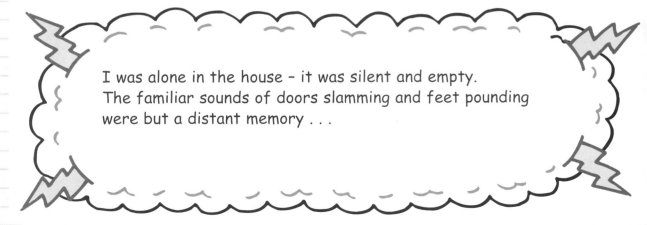

I was alone in the house – it was silent and empty.
The familiar sounds of doors slamming and feet pounding
were but a distant memory . . .

Start by brainstorming your ideas. This is a method many writers use to get their initial ideas on the page. Remember, all writers are scared of blank white paper – or blank computer screens!

Look at Helen's brainstorm for her short story *The House*. She has just scribbled down fragments of thoughts – they do not need to be written in proper sentences as they are just there to remind you of your ideas once you start writing.

Exercise 2

Now brainstorm your story *Alone* again as though it was another genre. If your first brainstorm was a mystery, for example, rewrite it as a science fiction story. Remember, write short notes on how your story goes, including any ideas you have, however 'way out'. Although you don't need to write your jottings in order, it can help to mark whereabouts, approximately, they come in the story to remind yourself of what happens!

RED ALERT RED ALERT RED ALERT RED

Collecting vocabulary

Understanding the jargon

A metaphor is a figure of speech in which a word or phrase is likened to something it does not literally denote.

Example

Her silken skirt whirled as she danced, butterfly wings gracefully wrapping around her.

Example

As black as a bat's wing.

A simile describes something by saying it is like something else. It often uses the words 'as' or 'like'.

Example

The car was a spirited girl dancing carelessly round the hairpin bends.

Personification is when human characteristics are given to non-human things.

Exercise 1

On page 23, you wrote a brainstorm for a fictional piece called *Alone*. Now you are going to collect some vocabulary and create similes, metaphors and personification to make your story more interesting. Try to write words and phrases that appeal to all of the reader's senses: sights, smells, sounds, tastes and physical feelings. Let your imagination create a 'film' in your head of the story as it unfolds.

Eerie open spaces
Neck prickling as though being watched

Similes:
Loneliness is like...

Metaphors:
The darkness was complete.
It was huge black...

Personification:
Loneliness stalked me like...

24

Collect words you like the sound of when you are reading to improve your writing. Keep a notebook computer file to do this.
A L

All writing is improved by using varied and exciting vocabulary, and this applies to both fictional and non-fictional writing.

Helen has written her brainstorm about *The House*.

> *Dappled light*
> *Clumps of dust*
> *Film of greasy brown dirt clinging to the windows, as though someone had smoked heavily in the room for years*
> *Iridescent*
> *Suffocating stench*

However, she is now moving on to develop her writing by collecting some interesting vocabulary. She has written examples of similes, metaphors and personification to make her words vivid and highly visual.

> **Metaphors**
> *The garden was a defence tactic, built by the house to keep out prying eyes.*
>
> **Similes**
> *The door of the house was like a huge iridescent beetle, scaling the front wall of the house. It bulged as though trying to contain something that desperately clawed at the unyielding surface, frantic to be free.*
>
> **Personification**
> *The house was a sullen old man, once grandly dressed but now fading, some long-forgotten humiliation causing an elegant fall from grace.*

Exercise 2

Write a simile to describe each of these things.

fierce cat
sleepy dog
fizzy sweets
juicy satsuma
blue sky
murky pond

> Fierce cat – like a spitting fire

Tactics

A simile is when something is LIKE something else.
A metaphor is when something IS something else.

25

Character profiling

When you create a character, it is important to make them real 3D people. If you just create sketchy characters with no depth, readers will not care about them and will lose interest in your story.

A useful device is a 'character profile'. This is a series of questions to ask yourself about the character you are creating. When the answers are combined, they give you a 'profile' of the character.

Helen has written a profile of a character called Isobel in her story about *The House*.

Exercise 1

Write a character profile for the main character of your story, *Alone*.
Use Helen's as a model.

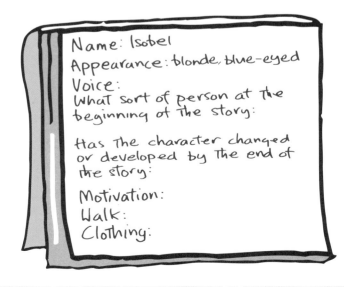

Name: Isobel
Appearance: blonde, blue-eyed
Voice:
What sort of person at the beginning of the story:

Has the character changed or developed by the end of the story:

Motivation:
Walk:
Clothing:

Try to visualise your character as you are thinking. You could base him or her on someone you know to make them believable.

My Character Profile   by Isobel Byrne

Name:	Isobel Byrne
Appearance:	Small, elfin-featured, long pale blonde hair. Small hands, well-kept nails.
Voice:	Low-toned voice, pleasant. Infectious laugh seems too big for her small frame.
At the beginning of the story:	Isobel seems a little shallow; very concerned about appearance. She is inquisitive, afraid of looking stupid.
Any character change or development by the end of the story:	Yes - fear, then her own bravery and discovery of the old woman make her think hard about what is important in her own life.
Motivation:	Nosiness and a sense of bravado; wanting to be accepted by a new crowd. Later, a growing sense of responsibility and tenderness for the woman.
Walk:	Dainty to begin with; later more purposeful.
Clothing:	Fashionable and neat, up-to-date. Nails painted with stencils.
Age:	Teenage girl
Situation/Mood:	Needing new friends; angry.

Exercise 2

Choose a book you have read recently, and write a profile for one of the characters. Comment on his or her:

- appearance
- voice
- character development
- walk
- motivation
- clothes
- age
- situation/mood

RED ALERT RED ALERT RED ALERT RED

Planning work

As you plan a story, think about the following questions to help you to build a framework and to structure your ideas.

Read Helen's framework for her story, *The House* (see page 23).

Where/when does your story begin?
In the street as Isobel walks off angrily from her friends.

Who is going to appear in your story (main characters)?
Isobel   a 14-year-old girl
Maude   an extremely elderly woman
Grendel   Maude's long-haired and rather fierce tabby cat

Do you have an exciting beginning to set the scene and make the reader want to continue?
Isobel's hands flexed into fists as she blustered along the road, angry with her friends. Before she knew it, she was far away from them, standing in front of the old Van Daemon house.
For as long as she could remember the house had sat there, derelict and empty. It was a sullen old man, once grandly dressed but now fading, some long forgotten humiliation causing an elegant fall from grace.

Exercise 1

Build a framework for your own story, *Alone*, by answering these questions.

1 Where does your story begin?

2 Who is going to appear in your story?

3 Do you have an exciting beginning to set the scene and make the reader want to continue?

4 How does the story develop? Do any major changes occur during the story?

5 Do you have a good strong ending? Is there a 'twist in the tail' of the story?

6 Is there a problem to solve?

RED ALERT   Try to 'get inside your characters' trainers and walk around for a bit'. Imagine what it would be like actually to be your character. How would you act?   **AL**

How does the story develop? Do any major changes occur during the story?

Isobel goes into the house to prove she isn't scared of anything - her friends have been teasing her because she won't ask a boy she likes out on a date. At first she's really scared; a cat jumps out on her, hissing and snarling like a dog. She hears noises in a room upstairs and finds a really elegant but incredibly old woman actually lives in the house. Over the course of the summer Isobel grows up a lot, helping the old woman to reconnect with people.

Do you have a good strong ending? Is there a 'twist in the tail' of the story?

No 'twist' here as such but Isobel comes to understand how her own life is in danger of echoing the loneliness of the old lady, Maude.

How does your story end?

The house had lost its air of elegant decay. Light streamed into the windows, revealing the rich jewel colours of exotic woollen textiles from far away, cinnamon-scented village bazaars.
The sound of running water from the fountain in the garden, flowing again now, mingled with the lilting of children's voices as they hid among the trees. Isobel slid her arm around her friend, and they walked slowly out into the afternoon sunshine.

Is there a problem to solve?

Not in the sense of there being a mystery, but Isobel's attitude has to change. Also, Maude is a recluse all alone at the beginning of the story, and this changes during the story.

Look how Helen has noted and ordered her ideas. Using planning notes like this can help you to keep track of your own plot and to make your story utterly captivating!

Exercise 2

Use the plan below to write a story.

Where does your story begin?
The Everglades swamp – mangroves
Who is in your story?
John, Jasbir and Dita
Do you have an exciting beginning?
The breeze was heavy with the warm smell of weed rotting in black mud.
How does the story develop?
Boys get lost in swamp – encounter alligator – seems to be following them. Find ancient holy place with shrine to reptilian god.
Do you have a good strong ending?
Once again, brooding quiet enveloped the swamp, but this time it was silence heavy with the secrets of its victims.

RED ALERT RED ALERT RED ALERT RED

1

Presenting your writing

- When you have written a wonderful story, it is important that readers are not put off by your presentation. At school and in tests, the content of your writing will be seen as the most important part of the writing process – but if your presentation is poor you will lose marks. Imagine having a choice between a scruffy old magazine that had been lying around in a waiting room, creased and covered in scribbles, or a pristine new magazine fresh from the shop with its free gift still attached. That's how teachers feel when they are faced with poorly presented work. Even if the content is great, the presentation can let work down.

- Presentation includes:
  - spelling
  - punctuation
  - organisation: paragraphs
  - organisation: sentences
  - handwriting

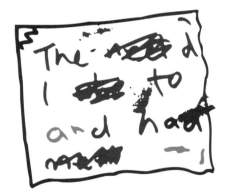

Handwriting

- Although many people use word–processing packages to 'write' today, neat handwriting is still an important skill. Basically, it doesn't matter how brilliant your work is if no one can read it!

- Handwriting as such is not usually taught at Key Stage 3, but teachers will often ask you to 'keep your work neat' or make comments about your presentation (or, rather, your lack of it!). They may even give you tips on improving your handwriting, talking about *ascenders, descenders, upper case* and other such obscure jargon.

The student's guide to 'teacher terms'

Teacher terms

Ascender:	this means the 'stick' on letters such as *b, d* and *h*.
Descender:	this means the 'tail' on letters such as *p, g*, and *y*
Upper case:	capital letters
Lower case:	all letters that are not capitals

Top tips for good handwriting

- Make sure you are sitting in a comfortable position when you are writing. If it helps, angle your page to make yourself comfortable.

- Make sure you are holding your pen comfortably with your index finger and thumb.

- Check your equipment – no one can do their best when they are writing with a leaky, scruffy old biro!

- Look at a recent piece of your own handwriting and ask yourself the following questions:

  Is the spacing between words and letters regular?

  Are letter joins regular and consistent – or do my letters join in different ways as I go through a passage?

  Are the letters the correct shape and size?

  Are my upper and lower letters in the correct proportion to one another?

  Are my ascenders and descenders the correct uniform length?

- Finally, do not despair. The best way to improve your writing is to keep practising. And you can take comfort from the fact that Shakespeare's 'penmanship' was pretty poor – and he did rather well for himself!

Structuring sentences

Words are organised into sentences to communicate ideas, and there are several types of sentence.

There are simple sentences that communicate one idea.

> ## Example
> Isobel was angry with her friends.

Exercise 1

Read this passage that Helen has written.

> A noise. Not a loud noise. But an insistent, scratching, 'I'm coming to get you' noise. From upstairs. Holding her breath, Isobel grasped the banister and set off up the stairs at a run, bounding and roaring as she climbed. She flew into the room, the door crashing against the wall with a resounding crack as she entered. She scanned the room feverishly, brandishing the poker in front of her like a talisman.
>
> And then she saw it, hissing and snarling in anger at the disturbance. A cat. Not even a particularly large cat. It stared at her, eyes glittering defiance. Then she heard a rustle from the dark recess by the window; a sound that vaguely reminded her of the time when she helped her mum to clear dry old leaves from the yard in the autumn.

Note how Helen has used a variety of sentence types to organise her story and to help build the mood. The passage begins with short, simple sentences which echo her feelings – she is afraid, and making small, quick movements. Isobel's headlong rush upstairs is contained in a complex sentence, which also mirrors the movements she makes – continuous, in a stream of words.

RED ALERT Read your work over to make sure that your sentences AL
flow together properly and make sense.

There are compound sentences that link two or more simple sentences using conjunctions such as *so*, *but* and *and*.

> ### Example
> Isobel was angry with her friends, so she stormed off down the street.

> ### Example
> Isobel was angry with her friends, so she stormed off down the street, looking for something to do on her own.

Then there are *complex sentences* that communicate several ideas, often separated by commas.

Exercise 1 continued

Now read the next part of the story.

Isobel was curious. She was also afraid. She stepped forward, timidly at first, then with growing confidence. It was probably just another cat, like the first. There was a sudden flare of light, and the sharp scent of paraffin. As her eyes adjusted to the light, Isobel found herself looking into the oldest face she had ever seen. The face looked even older than her grandad Maurice! Isobel gasped, and drew back like a turtle shooting backwards into its shell. A pair of red rimmed but intensely blue eyes regarded her with surprise, with a hint of amusement.

Comment on the sentences that Helen has used. Has she used:
• simple sentences?
• compound sentences?
• complex sentences?

Why do you think she chose the sentence structures in the way she did?

Organising work

Sentences are organised into chunks of writing called paragraphs. Paragraphs are used to give the reader a sign that something new is being introduced.

A new paragraph usually has its own topic. That does not mean that it does not link with the previous paragraph, but that each section usually has a new idea. Leaving a space of a line between the new paragraph and the old paragraph shows a new paragraph.

Example

(Paragraph 1)
The two ice skaters wirled and danced over the arena. They looked magical.
(Paragraph 2)
Suddenly, from the audience, came a loud bang.

Exercise 1

Read the passage below.

> *The ground was sloping downwards now, and becoming more and more like a rubbish dump. The air was heavy and full of smoke, and of other smells besides: acrid chemicals, decaying vegetable matter, sewage. And the further down they went, the worse it got. There was not a patch of clean soil in sight, and the only plants growing anywhere were rank weeds and coarse greyish grass.*
>
> *Ahead of them, above the water, was the mist. It rose like a cliff to merge with the gloomy sky, and from somewhere inside it came those bird cries that Tilly had referred to.*
>
> *Between the waste heaps and the mist, there lay the first town of the dead.*
>
> From The Amber Spyglass *by Philip Pullman*

Why do you think the author started new paragraphs? Continue the explanation below.

I think the author started a new paragraph to talk about the mist because it was a different thing than the rubbish and pollution he had been describing in the first paragraph. The third paragraph ...

Now read this passage.

The mud pots were hissing. Like obscene old men indulging in a ridiculous dance, they puffed up and popped with the slurp of toothless mouths blowing kisses.

David coughed as the sulphurous stench choked his breathing. He was used to the smell of the hot springs, but today he was distracted. He shifted uncomfortably as the memory of yesterday's trip into town flooded his mind, leaving him gasping like a fish on a slab.

Win had been his friend since they'd poked holes in ant nests together as kids, running away whooping as the furious creatures swarmed out, ready to fight invaders to the death. Win was part of the wallpaper that made up his childhood memories: in the creek – splashing Win. Cramming mouths full of fragrant watermelon, then pip-spitting competitions – with Win.

David replayed the events of yesterday over in his mind. Win and him had taken their bikes to the store to get some flour and sugar for Ma.

His mind wandered for a moment in a syrup scented memory of the sticky pancakes she had wanted to make.

They'd bought the provisions and left, then David had gone back into the store at the last moment to check if his dad's paper was in. When he'd come out of the store, he couldn't see Win, but he could see a gang of kids from the town in a circle. They were taunting something.

Exercise 2

Now read the next part of David's story. Put the text into paragraphs, remembering the points given above.

David hoped it wasn't one of the mangy pups that loitered around the store for the scraps thrown by Old Johnny as he cleared out at the end of the day. Suddenly, a clown appeared, bursting out of the circle with a blood-chilling yell. But it wasn't a clown. It was Win. And his beautiful chestnut skin, the colour of burnished copper, was clogged with the contents of his Ma's provisions bag. "Now you're the right colour to shop in Old Johnny's!" laughed a tall boy with unfeasibly short hair. It wasn't a pleasant laugh.

RED ALERT RED ALERT RED ALERT RED

Review your own work

When you have finished a piece of writing, always read your work back to yourself. Sometimes, in the frenzy of writing something you find really interesting (or in your hurry to get a piece of work finished), you can get distracted and write something that makes no sense at all!

These are the things to look out for:

- Does my work make sense in general terms?

- Have I answered the question I was asked – that is, 'How does the author create a feeling of loss and betrayal in this passage?' does not mean 'Tell us everything you know about the story. We will be really impressed that you have actually read it'.

- Is my work separated into paragraphs, or does it just tumble down the page in a torrent of consciousness?

- Do the tenses in my work flow correctly, or do I flip flap backwards and forwards from past to present and back again with all the continuity of a Dalek joyriding in Dr. Who's Tardis?

Exercise 1

Copy out and read the following passages. Mark where you think they could be improved.

1   I ~~like~~ chocolate cake more than any other cake in the world. A good chocolate cake ~~shoud~~ be moist and fragrant↑ crumbling easily as you bite it. ~~I like fudge frosting best of all~~.

    better word – adore
    spelling – should
    comma here
    better words – My favourite icing is chewy fudge frosting

2   I play in a band, rehersing at weekends and sometimes in the evenings. Sometimes we play at gigs orgenised by the community centre. We play mainly indie-pop but stray into rock sometimes.

3   My favourite animal is my cat. She is big and black.

4   My school plays lots of team games. Some of the team games the school is involved with are netball, rounders, football, hocky and basketball. My favrite team game is football becos I am very good at it and I like it a lot.

RED ALERT   Beware! Do the tenses flow well in your story or do   AL
they change from sentence to sentence? This is a very
common and extremely irritating mistake.

- Have I used punctuation correctly or does all my work just run together in really, really long sentences that don't really make sense and I would suffocate if I tried to read them out aloud as its very common for students to do this when they are concentrating hard on the content of their work but this makes ideas ambiguous and hard to understand . . . (Phew!)

- Have I checked that my vocabulary is varied, or do I drone on and on using the same word or words time after time?

- Hav I cheked my spelins proply?

- Is my work easy to read and is my writing legible?

Exercise 2

Read the passage below, then rewrite it with corrections. Consider the:

- paragraphs
- tenses
- punctuation
- spelling

Mewlius Caesar was the leeder of the colony of feral cats not as feirce or big as some of the others but a leader nevertheless. He was white with black patches that made him look as though he had knocked paint on his back. He loved to lay in the sun but never missed the opportunity to snuggle up to his human family. He was a grand old man and we miss him still.

Mewlius Caesar was the leader ...

2

Research skills

- Writers are often told to 'write about what you know'. That is fine if you know about lots of things, but could make life quite dull if all you know about is 'the fascinating life cycle of the bot fly'. Fine for one article, possibly, but after that ... perhaps not.

- You might well, however, be asked to write about a whole range of subjects that you know absolutely nothing about. This means you have to do some research.

- Research just means 'finding out about things'. Luckily, there are many ways of doing research.

  - Go to the library. The big building. With books. If you do a search (often on computer, but sometimes on microfiche or even on cards) and cannot find the things you are looking for, the librarian will be able to order things for you from other libraries, usually for a small fee.

  - Look in books at home. Depending on the subject matter, those encyclopedias may have a use after all.

– Search the internet. This vast, electronic library will definitely have what you are looking for. If you are not on the internet at home, try logging on at school, in a library, or in one of the many new internet cafés.

– Search CD–ROMs on relevant subjects.

– Ask your parents/grandparents/siblings. They may know something about the topic – or know a good place to find out.

• Once you have found a source of information, you need to make notes. Do not slavishly copy everything straight out of books or off the internet. Think about the question you are researching, and look for specific answers. If you are looking for reasons why rainforest ecosystems are important to the maintenance of the ozone layer, don't just write down everything you find  about rainforests. Research for this question could include:

– library archive footage of logging and deforestation
– videos of documentaries such as *Life on Earth*
– leaflets and booklets from the Friends of the Earth, the Worldwide Fund for Nature or Greenpeace
– an internet search, typing in *ozone layer* and *rainforest*.

• Make sure you have used a variety of sources for your research and make sure you list the resources you have used.

Writing for an audience

When you are writing, it is very important to be aware of the audience you are writing for. Once you are clear about this, you need to think about how to match your writing appropriately.

The following passage was written for children at primary school.

> *J is for Jilabi, a mouth-watering, crunchy yellow sweet. To make it, the sweet-maker presses chickpea flour batter through a mould into a deep pan of boiling oil to fry, until it looks like a fat spider's web. Then, after a dipping in sugar syrup, it is ready to eat.*
>
> *From* I is for India *by Prodeepta Das*

The writer, Prodeepta Das, matched his writing to his audience by:
• using appropriate language for children of this age – that is, not too complex;
• writing about subjects his audience would find interesting – sweets.

Exercise 1

Write a passage for children of the same age, about a toy you think they would find interesting. Remember the way Prodeepta Das matched his writing to his audience.

Exercise 2

Now rewrite your passage from exercise 1 so that it is appropriate for a different audience. You might aim it at a secondary school class or a village hall talk.

RED ALERT **Always be clear about your audience, and tailor your** **AL**
writing accordingly.

Now read this passage from *Blood Kiss*.

> *"OH, GROSS!" THAT WAS DELIA. EMPHATICALLY. Everything Delia did was emphatic. You could hear her coming a mile away. You knew her opinions right up front.*
>
> *"Eww ..." Valerie wasn't emphatic. In fact, Val was practically a disappearing act. Frail. Waiflike.*
>
> *Big eyes like on those hokey sympathy cards. Only she wasn't frail. Or waiflike. Not really.*
>
> *"No way." That was me. Chiming in as always. I'm Elizabeth. My parents named me Elizabeth along with hundreds of other kids from my generation. Dare to be the same ... I've tried to think of nicknames that might be distinctive.*
>
> *From* Blood Kiss *by D. E. Athkins*

Read Susie's comments. She has tried to identify the 'target audience', using clues such as the type of language used and the subject matter. Although this is a piece of fiction, the writing has still been matched to a particular audience.

> I think this writing is aimed at teenagers, girls in particular. There are references to common teenage girl behaviour (looking for a nickname; trying to be 'different', talking about boys); the slang and general language used ('hokey', 'gross' and 'eww!') is used by teenagers, and there is particular reference to the young woman's appearance and I think teenage girls in particular would notice her appearance in these terms.

Exercise 3

> *It was one of those things they keep in a jar in the tent of a sideshow on the outskirts of a little, drowsy town. One of those pale things drifting in alcohol plasma, forever dreaming and circling, with its peeled, dead eyes staring out at you and never seeing you. It went with the noiselessness of late night, and only the crickets chirping, the frogs sobbing off in the moist swampland. One of those things in a big jar that makes your stomach jump as it does when you see a preserved arm in a laboratory vat. Charlie stared back at it for a long time.*
> *From the short story,* The Jar, *in* The October Country *by Ray Bradbury (Rupert Hart-Davies, Soho Square, London 1957)*

Who do you think is the target audience? Give your reasons.

General spelling rules

Rules at home, rules at school – as though they weren't enough, now I've got to learn 'Spelling rules'!

Understanding the jargon

A prefix is a syllable or syllables with a set meaning that are added to the beginning of a word: *anti-* (meaning against) as in *anticlockwise*; *hyper-* (meaning over or excessive) as in *hyperactive*.
A suffix is a syllable or syllables with a set meaning which are added to the end of a word: *-ness* (*kind + ness = kindness*).
A plural is more than one: *dog/dogs, baby/babies*.
Vowels are the letters *a, e, i, o* and *u*.
Consonants are all of letters of the alphabet apart from the vowels.
A syllable is each unit of sound in a word as you say it is a syllable: *but/ter* has two syllables.

It will help your spelling if you learn some general rules; e.g. *i before e except after c*.

> **Example**
>
> Deceive and receive.
>
>

Exercise 1

Some of the words in the following sentence have been incorrectly spelled. Copy out the sentences, underline the incorrect words and give the correct spellings.

                    changeable   always   ladies   field

1. The weather was <u>changable</u>. As <u>allways</u>, the <u>ladys</u> were collecting the fruit from the <u>feild</u>.
2. The ladys admited that the marks on the cieling were the result of their football game.
3. The hotel submited a bill for the damage, which was quite noticable as the room was entered.
4. Untill the bill was setled, the ladys were not allowed to go home.

RED ALERT   Remember to learn these rules, and always to check your spellings at the end of your work.   AL

Words ending in silent *e* lose the *e* when the *-ing* or *-ed* suffix is added.
For example: Decide becomes deciding and decided.

Words ending in silent *e* keep the *e* if you need to keep the *s* or *j* sounds on words ending in *-ce* or *-ge*.
For example: change → changeable; manage → mangeable; service → serviceable

When the words full, well, all and till are added to the end of a word as a suffix or the beginning of a word as a prefix, they all lose one l.
For example: help + full → helpful;
all + ways → always; un + till → until

If a word ends in consonant + *y*, make it plural by changing the *y* into *ie* before you add *s*.
For example: baby → babies;
lady → ladies; pony → ponies

With a one-syllable word, double the last consonant before adding a suffix beginning with a vowel.
For example: mop + ing → mopping; pop + ing → popping; stop + ing → stopping;
top + ing → topping

With words of more than one syllable, look at the last syllable and treat it in the same way – that is, double the last consonant before adding a suffix beginning with a vowel.
For example: begin + ing → beginning; submit + ed → submitted;
admit + ed → admitted

Exercise 2

Write down and learn spelling rules, and make up some fun sentences to help you to remember spellings such as:

- There is a rat in separate
- I before e except after c.
- Make up mnemonics, such as Richard Of York Gave Battle In Vain to remember the colours of the rainbow (red, orange, yellow, green, blue, indigo, violet).

RED ALERT RED ALERT RED ALERT RED

Figurative language

By Key Stage 3, you are expected to be able to use figurative language in your descriptive writing. The most commonly used forms of this are similes and metaphors.

A simile is an obvious, open comparison that often uses the words *like*, *as* or *than*.

Examples

The day was fluid and warm, *like* molten chocolate.
The ladybird was as red and shiny *as* a cherry.

A metaphor is an implied, hidden comparison. Although the metaphor is not literally true, it is written as though it is.

Examples

The slug *was* a rubber comma, glistening in the sun.
The fish *was* a sliver of glass, slicing through the water.

Exercise 1

Read the sentences below and decide which contain similes and which contain metaphors. Write S (simile) or M (metaphor) for each one.

1   The sun was an orange, thrown into the sky by a playful child. (M – the writer says the sun was an orange).

2   The cat snored with a noise like the rumble of distant thunder, muffled by cloud.

3   The dragonfly was a crystal Spitfire, swooping over the heads of the bobbing sedge grass.

4   The car was as sluggish as an elderly camel, limping up the hill.

5   The wrinkles on her face were a road map, showing all the journeys, joyful and unhappy, that she had made.

6   The sky was as blue as a blackbird's egg.

7   The baby's ear was a tiny perfect shell.

RED ALERT   **If you are asked to comment on a piece of writing, make sure you identify and describe similes, metaphors and personification.**   **AL**

People often use similes and metaphors when they speak. These are usually clichés and should be avoided when you are writing. Similes and metaphors should be original and interesting.

Some clichés to avoid:
It's raining cats and dogs.
As dead as a dodo.
To be as good as gold.

Remember to look for interesting similes and metaphors when you are reading – poetry is often a good source.

Personification is another way to liven up your writing. It is a special type of metaphor where an inanimate object (one that has no life) is given a human form. This type of figurative language is also often used in poetry.

Examples

The trees were stately ladies, swaying in the warmth of the summer afternoon. Their leaves softly clapped, green-gloved hands, celebrating the cooling breeze.

Exercise 2

Write a sentence to personify each of these:

* winter
* a mountain
* snow
* the wind
* the sea
* spring
* the sun
* a wood
* a storm
* a warm beach

The winter was like an old man – grey-haired and wise.

RED ALERT RED ALERT RED ALERT RED

The author's craft

Authors use a variety of techniques to build the mood they wish to create. Read this passage.

> Then, suddenly, he had the strong, clear sense that someone was moving underneath him, hands pulling him down below the ground.
>
> *You are going to die,* said a voice in his mind. *Let me in. Give your body over to me.*
>
> Xander gasped. *I don't think so!*
>
> *What choice do you have?*
>
> "Xander!" Cordelia shrieked. "The ropes are burning!"
>
> *What do I do?* he thought.
>
> *Let me in, let yourself slip away. It will be like dying,* the voice told him.
>
> *But won't I die?* Xander asked.
>
> *If you would save her, act now,* it told him.
>
> Cordelia's screams were unbearable. Xander's mind, awash in pain, flashed past words to surrender.
>
> *Yes,* he thought. *Anything.*
>
> For just a second, he felt it, filling him up, a presence there with him, a mind ... and then he was gone. No more pain, no more monsters, no more fire. Only nothing. Cold and grey. Oblivion.
>
> *From* Immortal, *a novelisation of Buffy the Vampire Slayer by Christopher Golden and Nancy Holder (Pocket Books)*

Exercise 1

Choose a novel you have enjoyed reading. Read through the opening chapter again, then think about the mood of the story.

Has the author used:

*   special vocabulary?
*   particular sentence structure to build a mood?
*   speech to build suspense or mood?

Make brief notes to help you to organise your ideas.

The author has used several techniques.

- The thoughts of the character Xander, and the strange presence trying to possess him, are expressed in italics, without speech marks. This is in contrast to the character Cordelia's words, shown in ordinary script and with speech marks. The italicised text 'sounds' quieter as you read the story than it would have done if it had been written using speech marks. This suggests thoughts rather than spoken words.

- The short sentences used by Xander and the presence suggest an argument – a struggle of some sort. As Xander gives in to the presence, the author switches to a long flowing sentence.

For just a second, he felt it, filling him up, a presence there with him, a mind ... and then he was gone.

This suggests a surge as the ghostly presence rushes in to possess Xander.

Think about the way in which authors create moods as you read. It could be the language they use, or the way they structure sentences. When you answer exam questions, the ability to comment on techniques such as these will help you to achieve high marks. Better still, it will help you to understand and enjoy the books you read!

Write a passage full of suspense using the words in the box as a stimulus.
Try to use the techniques you read about in the piece from *Immortal*.

> breathless   silence   sudden stillness   racing pulse   tense
> jumpy   imagination   scraping sound   getting closer
> holding breath   slowly turning   grabbed

RED ALERT RED ALERT RED ALERT RED

A personal word bank

"I said hello, then she said hello and we went to the shops and said hello to the man behind the counter. He said hello to us and then we bought some sweets and said goodbye. He said goodbye to us as well... drone ... drone ... "

What a bore! If he'd said 'said' again, I would have exploded!

How many different words can you think of that mean *said*?

shrieked   whimpered

screeched

answered   replied   complained   wailed   screamed   demanded

asked

shouted   sobbed   roared   cried   whispered

yelled   commented   repeated   squealed   squeaked   bellowed

When you are writing, try not to repeat words as this makes your work dull and repetitive. Avoid this by building your own word bank. Collect words as you come across them, when you are reading and as you hear them on the television. This is better than copying words out of a thesaurus, which you may never use!

Write a passage to build a sense of horror using the words below.

screech   rattle   mist   brooding   whisper   bony fingers   skeletal

chill   alone   hideous   desolate   creak

> **Example**
>
> The door creaked open, hinges screeching as the old iron work moved ...

Exercise 1

Make a word bank for the following words.

1 walk – slouched, crept ...
2 small – tiny, minuscule ...
3 big – enormous, gigantic ...
4 run
5 sad
6 happy
7 make
8 go
9 nice
10 funny

RED ALERT   Try not to keep repeating the same words when you are writing – it makes your writing dull and boring!   AL

Hazel loves writing stories, and has made a collection of words in her notebook. She scribbles them down when she reads them, or when she hears them on television. Most of the words she collects are good to say, or have 'good mouth feel'. To find out what a good mouth feel is, try reading them aloud.

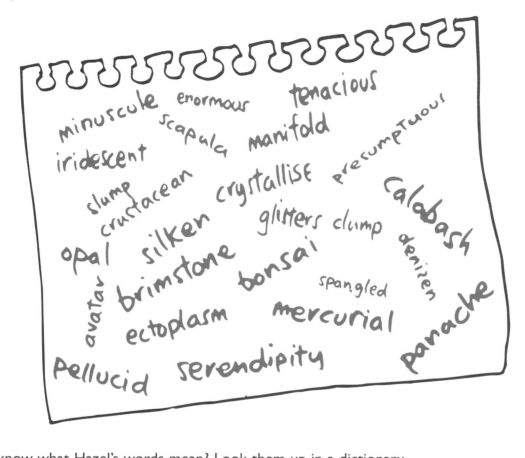

minuscule enormous tenacious
scapula manifold
iridescent
clump presumptuous
crustacean crystallise
opal silken glisters clump calabash
avatar brimstone bonsai denizen
ectoplasm mercurial
spangled panache
pellucid serendipity

Do you know what Hazel's words mean? Look them up in a dictionary.

Exercise 2

Make your own collection of words with good 'mouth feel'. You might like to organise your pages under different headings so that they are easy to find when you are writing about a particular subject.

- weather
- plants
- animals
- feelings
- colours
- names

Skimming and scanning text

The ability to read quickly and to extract the information you need becomes essential at Key Stage 3 as you are often given large amounts of text to read.

When you are given a passage to read and answer questions about, read through quickly, skimming through the text. Read the question or questions and then scan through the text again, looking for key words that relate to your question. In a test or exam you could highlight or underline the text that seems relevant, to save time rereading the whole passage. Ensure you mark any phrases for quotations that support your answer.

Exercise 1

Read the poem at the top of page 51. Why did the poet choose to use cats as imagery in the poem?

Remember:
- Read the poem through quickly;
- Read it again, underlining any words or phrases relevant to the question;
- Use quotations from the poem to back up your answers.

tabby - more than one colour
colours change in autumn

Try to remember to use 'technical' words, such as similes and metaphors, when you write about imagery in poems.

He came in tabby September
When the fair shrieked on the hill,
Stood on the classroom threshold,
Stray cat on our window-sill.

His gold eyes begged for a welcome,
For milk and a place at our fire
But his thin frame remembered over
    arm stones,
Claws that tore like barbed wire.

In the yard after milk, in chrysanthemum sun,
We watched, domestic as cream.
The gipsy-boy, single, stood clenched by the
    fence,
Dark as a midnight dream.

We did not claw, nor spit nor hiss,
Yet we never invited him in,
Closed all our windows to with a thud,
Slammed each of our doors on him.

Traveller's Child by Jacqueline Brown

Sunil has read the poem through once quickly and noted words that will help him to answer the question: 'How do we know what season of the year it is when the travelling child visits?'

He has written:

The 'traveller's child' came to the school in the Autumn. The poem talks of 'tabby September', and September is in the autumn. The word 'tabby' conjures up mental pictures of mixed, changing, dappled colours like those seen in the autumn as the leaves change. The sun is described as a 'chrysanthemum', and these flowers bloom in the autumn.

Exercise 2

'Traveller's Child' is not a comfortable poem to read as we think about the child who wants to be accepted but is shunned by the village children. Which words in the poem create a sense of tension?

His gold eyes begged for a welcome . . .

Exercise 3

Choose a poem or piece of prose and read it through once, quickly. Make a note of everything you remember. Then read through the passage again slowly and check if you missed anything. This exercise will help you to develop your memory.

Reading between the lines

Poems – and sometimes prose writing – often have veiled or hidden meanings beyond the obvious. To discover this meaning we have to develop the ability to read 'between the lines' to understand the imagery used by the author.

Read the poem through several times so that you understand it.

> My son age three fell in the nettle bed.
> 'Bed' seemed a curious name for those
>   green spears,
> That regiment of spite behind the shed:
> It was no place for rest. With sobs and tears
>
> The boy came seeking comfort and I saw
> White blisters beaded on his tender skin.
> We soothed him till his pain was not so raw.
> At last he offered us a watery grin,

Exercise 1

Now read the following poem, 'Champion' by Robert Morgan.

> Billy was a marble champion
> With cord for a belt
> And elbow holes in his jersey.
>
> We played an hour before school
> On the concrete playground.
> But he dashed all our glassies
>
> Out of the chalk ring,
> Then he'd sell his winnings
> And buy breakfast at lunchtime.

What is the poem about? Is there one meaning, or can you identify more than one? Why do you think the poet calls Billy a *champion*? Give your reasons.

**Responding to poetry is a very personal thing – there   A |
are not always 'correct' answers to questions.**

And then I took my billhook, honed
    the blade
And went outside and slashed in fury with it
Till not a nettle in that fierce parade
Stood upright anymore. And then I lit

A funeral pyre to burn the fallen dead,
But in two weeks the busy sun and rain
Had called up tall recruits behind the shed:
My son would often feel sharp wounds
    again.

Nettles *by Vernon Scannell from* Mastering the Craft

Kevin read the poem, and then answered this question: 'On one level, this poem is about the poet's son being stung by nettles. Can you read between the lines to find a deeper meaning?'

Kevin says:

All the way through, the poem seems to just be an account of the little boy falling into a clump of nettles. But when you get to the last line, 'My son would often feel sharp wounds again', it makes you wonder if there is some deeper meaning. The last few lines could just mean that nettles keep growing, and a little boy may keep falling into them. But it could also mean that no matter how hard the poet tries, as a father, to keep his son from harm and hurt, there will always be new challenges to face, and the little boy will always be vulnerable to different 'sharp wounds'.

Exercise 2

Read this poem by Grace Nichols.

Like a Beacon

In London
Every now and then
I get this craving
For my mother's food
I leave art galleries
In search of plantains
Saltfish/sweet potatoes

I need this link

I need this touch
Of home
Swinging my bag
Like a beacon
Against the cold

From I'd Like to be a Teabag and Other Poems *from* Talking Poetry *by BBC Radio*

Can you read between the lines? What was Grace Nichols trying to tell the reader?

Persuasive writing

When you write an argument you are required to present and develop a particular point of view.

Read the leaflet below. It has been written by a group who want to persuade people that their view is correct.

But my mum tells me off for arguing!

RAP MUSIC SHOULD BE BANNED!

Rap is one of the most obscene, aggressive forms of popular music on the scene today. It is filled with drug imagery, the degradation of Women and violent images of ghetto life, the lyrics encourage anarchic behaviour of the kind.

PARENTS AGAINST RAP call for this disgusting music to be banned from our airwaves and stores. It is anti-family, anti-authority and respectability, and anti-religious.

STOP THE ROT NOW!

Exercise 1

Read the poster below, taken from a butcher's window. Then write your own argument against eating meat.

To present an argument:
• Organise yourself. Make a list of ideas.
• Be positive and sound certain that you are right – be prepared to exaggerate to make your point.

> ### MEAT IS GOOD FOR YOU!
> If you eat meat every day, it will make you strong and healthy.
> Without meat, you will not get all the vitamins you need.
>
> **A steak a day will keep anaemia away!**

54

Alexander and Jane have discussed the leaflet, and have come up with their own argument in favour of rap music.

We think that PARENTS AGAINST RAP are wrong. Rap music can be soulful, poetic and deeply meaningful. The songs are sometimes about drugs and violence, but these are often condemned. The rappers are singing about real life in very poor, disadvantaged areas – so the songs reflect this.

On some sleeve notes for 'OG', Ice-T says:

'No one lives in the ghetto by choice. Go to school, build your brain, ESCAPE THE KILLING FIELDS!!' This is the opposite of the viewpoint that PARENTS AGAINST RAP associate with rap artists.

Many rappers give a great deal back to their communities, investing money and time in projects to take young people off the streets, where they are at risk of involvement in crime and violence – and even gang membership.

On the track 'Life Is So Hard' (from the album 'Scorpion'), Eve thanks her family and God for her success, in a rapped prayer saying:

'Every day I pray to God ... I appreciate every blessing.'

She describes her love of God, and the way she thanks him for giving her strength every day to be the best person she can be.

We think, therefore, that it is unfair for PARENTS AGAINST RAP to say that all rap is a bad influence and should be banned.

Exercise 1 continued

• Use questions to make your points where there can only be one possible answer.
  For example: 'Surely we do not agree that animals should suffer so that we can enjoy a bacon sandwich?'
• Keep any criticism impersonal and do not make direct attacks on your opponents as it makes you sound aggressive and unreasonable.

Exercise 2

Now design a poster to persuade people to become vegetarians. Use the points you have noted in Exercise 1 to ensure your poster is strong, dynamic and to-the-point.

Planning non-fiction writing 1

Understanding the jargon

A brainstorm is an initial list of ideas as they occur to you and are not organised at first. Before you start to write your article, you may find it helpful to map out your ideas into some sort of linked order.

There are similarities between the tools used for planning fiction and non-fiction writing. As with writing fiction, brainstorming is a good starting point.

Here is a brainstorm Jaya has written for some ideas for a magazine article about the importance of wildlife gardening.

- wildlife corridors   • animals moving from place to place
- decline in wild habitat   • intensive farming, house building programmes
- pleasure factor   • seeing hedgehogs, frogs, bats close up
- fall in population   • frogs, slow worms, toads
- extinction   • butterfly/moth species   • see Butterfly Conservation Society

Exercise 1

You are going to write an article on the importance of clean beaches, both as marine habitats and places for human recreation. Write your own brainstorm of ideas.
Think about:
- What creatures live on the beach?
- Why are beaches dirty?
- How do we know beaches are dirty?
- How does litter/pollution affect creatures?
- How can we help to clean up the beaches?
- Are there organisations we can contact to find out more?

Exercise 2

Once your brainstorm has been completed, you need to organise your ideas. Decide which points you think would make the most impact in your article and put that first. Make a brief plan of paragraphs to help you to get organised.

Vivid descriptions, punctuation, grammar and spelling are as important in non-fiction writing as they are in story writing. A L

After finishing her brainstorm notes, Jaya prepared a paragraph plan to help her to link her ideas together. Read her paragraph plan.

For example, Jaya organised her brainstorm as follows:

Paragraph 1: write about a particularly beautiful creature - dragonfly? Talk about how they were common when I was little, but less so now - back up with facts from Wildlife Trusts info.

Paragraph 2: extinction - give some examples; decline in populations.

Paragraph 3: reasons- habitats destroyed, etc.

Paragraph 4: importance of wildlife corridors (and explanation of what they are).

Paragraph 5: what wildlife gardening means and how it can help.

Paragraph 6: contacts, such as Wildlife Trusts - list of local numbers; list of useful books.

Consider how Jaya has planned her article. Notice how she has organised the paragraphs into a logical order – in effect, she is telling a story from start to finish.

Exercise 3

Now use your brainstorm and notes to make a paragraph plan for your own article.

Exercise 4

Think of a subject you find interesting – it could be a hobby, such as model making, a sport, music ... whatever takes your fancy. However, it needs to be a subject you know well.

Write a brainstorm for an article to encourage people to find out more about your subject for a magazine. Then make a paragraph plan and write the article. Why not try to submit it to your school or youth club magazine?

RED ALERT RED ALERT RED ALERT RED

Planning non-fiction writing 2

You should have written a brainstorm for a magazine article and organised your ideas into a paragraph plan. Now you need to think about the style in which to present your ideas. The language you use and the layout you decide upon for your article will influence the way in which people feel as they read it.

Jaya has made two attempts at writing her first paragraph. Read the two versions, and decide which you prefer.

> Version one:
> Dragonflies are beautiful. It is a shame that there are less of them about today then when I was little. The local Wildlife Trust told me that it is because lots of ponds are being filled in.

Exercise 1

Write your own introductory paragraph for your article about clean beaches. Can you engage the feelings of the reader in the same way as Jaya?

Exercise 2

Once you have written your first paragraph successfully, try to complete your article using the paragraph plan you made. As you write, try to think of ways to lay out your article to make it interesting. Avoid having too much text close together because this can put some readers off. Can you make the important points stand out using devices such as bullet points, bold first sentences and illustrations? Look at a variety of magazine articles to give yourself ideas.

RED ALERT   Remember, emotive language can be a very effective   AL
tool when you are writing to persuade people.

Version two:

I remember my father taking me to Waterhall Valley most weekends when I was small. There was a huge, mossy pool flanked with bullrushes where we used to sit and gasp at the aerial displays given by the miniature, glittering dragons that buzzed over our heads. Even the names of the dragonflies were magical to me: azure hawker, ruddy darter, keeled skimmer. Today that pool is gone, and so are the iridescent beauties that lived there, banished by the black asphalt of the new municipal car park.

The second paragraph is more interesting, because it gives us descriptions and tells us about the importance of the issue to Jaya. She uses her emotions to engage our own and, because of her description, we feel a sense of loss because the pool has gone.

She uses words such as *banished* to refer to the dragonflies. This gives a sense of the creatures being sent away dramatically by the development of the park.

Her vivid descriptions of the antics of the dragonflies that made her gasp help to create a strong visual image in our minds. We can imagine how wonderful the dragonflies looked, and so share her sense of sadness that they have gone.

When she describes the names of the dragonflies as *magical*, she creates the feeling that they were special and precious – and should have been cherished.

Exercise 3

Read the words below. Which word in each trio is the most 'emotive' word – that is, which provokes the strongest feelings in the reader?

> What a nice/pleasant/glorious day.
> What a glorious day.

1 You've cut/hacked/pruned down my favourite tree!
2 There's no need to shout/bellow/scream.
3 I wish you would stop whining/talking/moaning.
4 That dog's smelly/dirty/stinking.
5 It's cold/chilly/arctic.

RED ALERT RED ALERT RED ALERT RED

Writing a speech

Sometimes, in order to answer a question in a test, you may be asked to write a speech to persuade your audience to take a particular viewpoint. If you listen to speeches and debates on the television or radio – perhaps given by politicians or other group leaders – it is possible to identify several useful strategies and techniques.

Mobile phones are a part of everyday life. Nowadays, everyone carries them, from young children to the elderly. Yet pupils at this school are denied this basic right! Do teachers think we will stop listening to their classes because we are too busy texting each other? Do they not care about our personal safety? A recent report in the Daily Blah told how a young girl was forced off a bus by a heartless driver because she did not have the correct fare. Luckily for her, she had a mobile phone in her bag and was able to ring her mother and be picked up safely. Had she been without a phone, she would have been marooned, alone in the dark, miles from home. Who knows what might have happened to her!

Mobile phones would help the school to run smoothly. How many times has a forgotten PE kit, text book or lunch made it necessary to phone home? How many times a day are office staff disturbed for these very phone calls? How much do these phone calls cost the school every year? Allowing the use of mobile phones in school would avoid all these problems and upheaval.

I firmly believe that the day will come when the voices of the student body of this school will be heard and accepted by the school administration. When that day comes, and mobile phones are allowed in school, we will be able to breathe a collective sigh of relief that will be echoed by our parents. When that day comes, we will always be able to contact our parents; we will feel safe again.

Exercise 1

Look at the speech above in favour of having mobile phones. Consider for example:
- Has it been well organised?
- Has the choice of words helped get the points across?
- Does the piece sound convincing?
- Who is being addressed?
- Does it finish strongly?
- Have you gained a clear picture of what the writer is talking about?

Make notes about the emotive language and describe the way in which the strong ending is effective.

RED ALERT Remember to write your speech so that it appeals to the particular audience you are addressing. AL

Useful techniques

- Organise information in logical order. Identify the issue, then talk about how it should be addressed.

- Use 'emotive' words – that is, words that are likely to create a strong response in the audience.

- Speak with an air of authority and knowledge of the subject.

- Tailor the speech to the particular audience being addressed.

- Ask rhetorical questions – that is, questions that do not really require an answer but are used to make people think in a certain way.

- Use repetition. This is a powerful technique that reinforces and 'underlines' points being made.

- Finish with a strong ending that sums up the main points of the speech and helps people to remember the ideas.

Exercise 2

Read the speech again, using the checklist at the top of the page to help you to decide how effective it has been.

Exercise 3

Write your own speech to persuade your audience that teenagers should be entitled to a grant whilst they are at school to pay for books, clothes and entertainment. Remember to use the techniques described in the box above.

Exercise 4

Listen to a speech given by a politician on the television or radio. Make a note of any of the techniques used that are described in the box above. Was the speech persuasive? How? Why? Why not?

3

Homework

Homework – who needs it? You do!

- Contrary to popular belief, teachers do not hand out homework because they are hideous creatures who like to torture children. Homework is actually set to help to make your life at school easier – to help you to understand topics and to give you practice in completing essays and exam questions. There are, however, things you can do to make homework more manageable.

- Make a note of homework as it is set – not later, as you may forget some of the details. Many schools give their students 'homework diaries' for this purpose. If yours does not, buy yourself a small notebook to use instead. Note down the date the homework is set, the date to hand it in and then details of work to be carried out.

- Organise yourself. Your teacher will not accept an excuse about not taking the correct textbook or exercise book home! Make sure you also have any equipment you need such as paper, reference books, access to the computer for word processing or internet searches.

- Make sure you understand the work you have been set. Your teacher will explain it to you again if you do not – it's their job, so don't be shy! Once you are at home in your bedroom and the homework is due the next day, it will be too late.

- Create a 'homework haven'. You may be lucky enough to have a desk in your bedroom. If so, make sure you have sufficient light and space to work. A desk buried under old sweet wrappers, magazines and furry coffee mugs is not a good place to work! If you do not have a desk, talk to your parents about the best place for you to do your homework. They may be able to make sure that you have a space at the kitchen table and peace and quiet to do your homework.

- Keep a timetable of your activities. You could even make a large copy for your wall!

- Plan your homework well in advance and you will have time to complete it and still enjoy all of your usual activities and free time!

	Monday	Tuesday	Wednesday	Thursday	Friday
activities & clubs	dance class 5-6.30pm		football practice 5.30-7pm		youth club 6-8pm

Reading aloud

- Shrinking violet or budding TV presenter – we are all called upon to take part in that dreaded school ritual of reading aloud! Although there will always be those irritating people in every class that seem desperate to be chosen to read aloud (and they don't seem to make mistakes, either) most students feel slightly nervous about reading to the class. There are some techniques that can make this 'ordeal' easier to bear.

- Try to stay calm. Although this is far easier to say than to do, a few deep breaths before you start will help to relax you.

- Imagine that you are just reading to yourself, or a younger brother or sister. Forgetting your audience will make you feel much more at ease.

- Without puffing as if you've just run up twelve flights of stairs, take plenty of breaths as you read. Use full stops and commas to guide you.

- Remember to read slowly enough for people to hear you properly. You don't need to sound as though you need winding up, but a common mistake when reading aloud (especially when you are nervous) is to read quickly, or even to speed up as you go.

- Remember to position yourself so that people can hear you. If your head is hanging down, looking at your boots, your voice will seem muffled. Try to keep your head level.

- Don't fiddle with your hair, twist your fingers or use any other 'nervous fidget' you can think of! If your body acts nervously, you will convince yourself to be nervous. Take a few moments to relax your muscles if you feel tense.

- If your throat feels tight as you prepare to read, and you think your voice will sound choked or squeaky, imagine you are about to eat a particularly huge and delightful strawberry. This will have the effect of taking your mind off your nerves, making your previously dry mouth water, and will relax your tongue and throat expectantly. (That is, of course, if you like strawberries!)

- And finally, practise, practise, practise – in front of family, friends, the mirror, the cat … the more you read aloud, the more natural it feels.

Drama

Life's a TV set, and all the people are merely soap stars ...

The word drama may conjure up a variety of images for you – crusty, boring old plays you are dragged along to by school, the ritual humiliation you endure when forced to take part in school productions, or the reaction your mum has to your suggestion that you get your nose pierced. Of course, you may love drama and know that the only thing you want to do when you leave school is to be an International Film Star – so you don't need careers advice, thank you!

Whichever view you take, drama is a part of the English curriculum and you will study it at school.

Drama, and the plays you study, have a particular vocabulary of their own:

- Acts – big sections of a play. These are like separate 'episodes' of the story.

- Scenes – smaller segments of the play. If a story moves on to a different place, or time passes, there is usually a new scene.

Exercise 1

The next time you watch your favourite soap, remember that it is in fact a type of televised play you are watching. Each episode could perhaps be called an *act*. Video an episode of the soap and play back a small part. Try to write the 'script' as the action unfolds. Remember to add stage directions (who does what and goes where) as well as dialogue.

Comment on the way that the words spoken by the characters help to create the mood the writer wanted. Could the writer have used more interesting or effective language?

RED ALERT If you learn the technical terms used when talking about plays, this will help you to comment on the action in a knowledgeable manner. **AL**

- Characters – the people in the play.

- Script – the words that tell the story; the words the actors speak.

- Stage directions – what the actors have to do.

In a play, here are no long explanations or descriptions as you would read in a novel – the only way we, the audience, get to know that something has happened is by seeing what the actors do or hearing what they say.

In your English lessons, you will be required to study and analyse plays as well as actually reading them out and acting them. Don't forget to comment on the type of language used, such as similes or metaphors, much as you would when discussing a poem or story.

You should think about the way in which the language has been used to create a feeling or mood, and the way that the imagery used contributes to this.

Exercise 2

Be the director!

Read an act from a play you are studying at school, or continue to use the 'script' from your soap video. Imagine that you are the director of the episode. It is your job to make sure that everything in the episode or scene runs smoothly and makes sense.

Make notes about the actions you would ask the actors to carry out, and the directions you would give them ain order to make the episode or scene interesting. Include notes about details such as mood, facial expression and body language.

RED ALERT RED ALERT RED ALERT RED

Story endings

Understanding the jargon

Genre is a type of writing, such as romance, science fiction, horror, humour.
The précis is a condensed summary.

When planning a story, you thought about an exciting opening passage to 'hook' your reader and make them want to read more. It is equally important to think carefully about the ending of your story. It is often the end of a story that people remember, especially if it was unexpected.

Types of endings:

- Endings with a sense of closure – a satisfying ending that ties up loose ends.
- Suspense – an ending with questions 'hanging in the air', so that the reader thinks about the characters and wants to hear more.
- The unexpected – a shocking ending, leaving the reader feeling unsettled. This often occurs in books from the horror or suspense genres.
- An emotional ending – happy or sad.

Exercise 1

Read this précis of a story, and its two alternative endings. Which do you prefer? Why? Give your reasons.

A starship has landed on an unmapped planet and the crew has been slaughtered one by one. The creatures carrying out the killings have cornered the last two crew members in a damaged space pod.

> ### Ending one:
> Alex sealed the pod door as the long talons reached inside, clawing at his pale face. Fitchett grunted with effort as he heaved at the control panel, urging the engines into life. With a cough, that grew into a growl and then a bellow the pod lurched forward. Still the obscene creature hung on, flailing suckered tentacles that slurped and pulsed against the glass of the main screen. The pod gained speed and shot into the air, climbing abruptly. The screams of the rushing air beating against the sides of the pod mingled with the shrieks of the abomination they carried. As they left the planet's atmosphere, a phosphorescent glow encased the pod. The creature started to writhe and shudder, then released its hold. The two men watched in silence as she wheeled off into the darkness, a silent scream etched on her features. All was calm.

This ending has been taken from *I am David* by Anne Holm. The main character in the book is a boy who has been imprisoned in a Nazi concentration camp and has lost his family. He escapes and travels alone across Europe in search of a place where he can feel safe and as though he belongs to someone.

> *French was the language he spoke best. David picked up his bundle, walked to the door and rang the bell. When the woman opened it, he knew she was the woman in the photograph, the woman whose eyes had seen so much and yet could smile.*
>
> *Then David said in French, "Madame, I'm David. I'm ... "*
>
> *He could say no more. The woman looked into his face and said clearly and distinctly, "David ... My son David ... "*

The reader has become caught up in David's story as it is so well written. The ending is satisfying because David has been alone for so long that he has begun to lose hope and the reader fears that he will give up. When he is unexpectedly reunited with his mother, the reader is caught up in a surge of happiness and the ending is extremely satisfying.

Exercise 1 continued

> **Ending two:**
> Alex sealed the pod door as the long talons reached inside, clawing at his pale face. Fitchett grunted with effort as he heaved at the control panel, urging the engines into life. With a cough, that grew into a growl and then a bellow the pod lurched forward. Still the obscene creature hung on, flailing suckered tentacles that slurped and pulsed against the glass of the main screen. There was a sound like ice cracking as the glass began to craze.
> "God help us!" shrieked Alex as the screen ballooned inwards, pausing before exploding in a starburst of glinting shards. With a guttural sigh of pleasure, the creature heaved itself into the pod. Then there was silence.

Exercise 2

Read some story endings. (Short stories are a good source to find a variety of endings.) Note down those stories you have read and whether the endings are dramatic and memorable, or whether they give a neat sense of closure. Which are your favourite endings? Why?

Reading non-fiction

Newspapers carry a variety of articles describing and reporting on events. They try to tell stories as briefly as possible. Typically, reports contain these features:

- A headline – to catch the reader's eye and encourage them to read the story.

- A topic sentence – usually the first sentence of the report, this tells you what the story is about.

- Short paragraphs – to help readers to skim quickly down the page. It is often thought, especially by tabloid newspapers, that people will be put off reading stories if there are dense, long blocks of text.

- Quotations – the words of people who are interviewed for the articles are often quoted directly, to give an air of truth and reality to stories.

When you read non-fiction, such as a newspaper report, you need to be able to:

- find ideas and information
- identify the purpose of the text – that is, what is the writer trying to achieve
- comment on the effect of particular words, phrases and layout.

Exercise 1

Choose a newspaper article that interests you. Write what you think the writer is trying to achieve and what you notice about the use of language.

- Identify the purpose of the text
- Comment on imagery
- What emotive language has been used? Is it effective?
- Is the layout of the article attractive and easy to read?

RED ALERT Look for puns in headlines – they are often used to engage the reader. A

Read the story below, about the environmental initiative called *Project 2000*.

Rabbits give ecologists a thumping headache

Caught on the hop as bunny army digs in

BURROWING bunnies have forced ecologists to scrap a green initiative which won praise from Prince Charles.

Ambitious plans had been drawn up for a series of walks to be developed along a mineral railway line.

Walkers would have been shown the wealth of wild flowers in the area on the walks which were to have run throughout the summer.

But at the last moment project co-ordinator and event organiser Alan Savage noticed the burrowing of the rabbits had undermined the wild flower habitats and made it unsafe for walkers.

He said: "Visitors can see a wealth of flora on the east-west mineral line, such as moonwort, wild daffodils, and orchids.

"However, rabbits have derailed the plans because their burrowing has caused subsidence.

"The old railway line is an area not used much by the public but it has been landscaped over the years and the walks would have encouraged ecotourism.

Collapse

"But because the rabbits have been down there for donkeys' years, the burrows are causing the land to collapse.

"It has made it unsafe for people to walk down there so the whole thing has been cancelled with no prospects of normal service being resumed.

"I've even been down there with my lurcher but they are burrowing into the embankment and it's virtually impossible to get rid of them."

The plans were the latest in a long line of imaginative ideas from the award-winning Cramlington Project 2000 in the Northumberland town's east end.

Plants gathered from around the world are saved and propagated by the volunteers who run the project.

And it is their work, which has helped them win both the Northumbria in Bloom and Blyth Valley in Bloom competitions, praise from the Prince and other members of the Royal Family.

Zachary has read the article and has answered the following questions: 'What do you think the writer is trying to achieve? What do you notice about the use of language?'

The writer is telling the audience about the problems Project 2000 are having with establishing a wildflower meadow because of rabbits burrowing under the site. The writer is also making a bit of a joke, as in pun about rabbits and the noise they make in the sentence 'Rabbits give ecologists a thumping headache'. I think he is also making a subtle reference to the 'eco-warriors' who have made tunnels and lived in trees to stop roads being built in the headline, which reads: 'Caught on the hop as bunny army digs in'.

Exercise 2

Use the brief below to write a newspaper article. Remember to think of a catchy headline and to consider the layout of your article.

Toad crossings have been built under roads and signs put up to warn motorists that toads cross the roads at particular points and may be injured. Thousands of toads killed every year as they move to water to spawn. Witness statement from Mrs Dench, resident of Stoneleigh Park – large country estate backing on to lake – it is appalling in spring. The poor little souls appear in their hundreds to breed and are cut down in their prime by cars zooming along who don't even notice the carnage they create.

RED ALERT RED ALERT RED ALERT RED

Grammar

Understanding the jargon

Ambiguity is when a meaning is unclear – where words could mean more than one thing, such as the pronouns *he*, *she* and *it*.

Have you noticed how things don't make sense if the words are not in the right order? Grammar, along with punctuation, is a way of making sure we organise our writing so that other people can understand us. Grammar is the way in which we organise language into sentences and paragraphs.

Example

My cat ate the fish because it was naughty.
This sentence is ambiguous. Was the cat naughty because it ate the fish, or did the cat eat the fish to punish it because it had done something naughty?

Example

'This is my M65 games console' is grammatically correct – it makes sense.
'My this M65 games console is' is not grammatically correct and it does not make sense.

Exercise 1

Read these sentences. Rewrite them so that they are no longer ambiguous.

1   The firefighter put on his protective hat because it was hot.
    – The fire was hot, so the firefighter put on his protective hat.
2   The woman stroked the cat because she was beautiful.
3   The boy hugged the dog because he was afraid.
4   The crab ate the whole fish, because it was huge.
5   If that baby doesn't want its milk, throw it away.
6   The leak was repaired before any damage was done by the woman.

72

Always read your work back to yourself to make sure it makes sense. It is easy to get carried away as you write and the ideas are flowing! Students often write sentences that make sense to them but whose meaning is not clear to the reader. One of the most common mistakes is to make the meaning of a sentence ambiguous. When a sentence is ambiguous, the reader has no way of knowing what the author meant. Sentences are often ambiguous because a word or phrase is in the wrong position. Ambiguity can also occur when pronouns are used in careless way, and it is unclear to whom they refer.

The boy picked up the mouse because he was injured.

This sentence is ambiguous because the pronoun 'he' has been used carelessly and it is not clear whether the 'he' referred to is the boy or the mouse.

Now read these ambiguous statements.

- The tiger ate the antelope because it was hungry.
  Who was hungry – the tiger or the antelope?

- The teacher roared at the girl because she was horrible.
  Who was horrible – the teacher or the girl?

- The mother told off her child because she was naughty.
  Who was naughty – the mother or the child?

- The nurse tucked the patient in tightly because he was cold.
  Who was cold – the patient or the nurse?

Exercise 2

Read the short, simple sentences below. Can you rewrite them to deliberately make their meaning ambiguous? It's harder than it sounds!

1 The dog ate the meat. The dog was brown.
   The dog ate the meat because it was brown.
2 The girl liked the horse. The horse was beautiful.
3 The boy cut his finger on the knife. The knife was sharp.
4 The mouse ate the cheese. The cheese was smelly.
5 The bat flew into the window. The window was transparent.
6 The elephant squirted the tree with water. The water was green and slimy.

5

Preparing for optional tests

- The bad news first. Unfortunately, the tests are optional for schools, but not for pupils. If your school adopts them, and most will, you have no choice. Now the good news. This book will help you to be really well prepared!

If they're optional, I don't want to do them!

- **R**evise sensibly. Start your revision in plenty of time so that you can do a 'little and often'.

- **E**ssential facts. Write shortened notes in a notebook as you revise so you can read them over quickly. This only works as a reminder if you have learned the work already!

- **D**on't rush into the questions without planning your answer. A few notes will actually save you time and help you to organise your ideas.

- **A**lways plan your time carefully. Don't spend ages on one question because you can answer it really well if it means you will run out of time on other questions.

- **M**ake sure you answer the question. If the question says, 'Why did Lady Macbeth go mad? How did Shakespeare convey her descent into madness to the reader?' do not just see the words 'Lady Macbeth' and write everything you know about her.

- **B**reak your notes up into 'bitesize chunks'. Trying to learn huge quantities of work all at once will probably confuse you.

- **E**nsure you get enough sleep, eat properly and have time to relax in the run up to the tests. If you are healthy and rested you will be able to do your best work.

- **R**ead the questions thoroughly. When you have a choice, answer the questions.

- **G**ather together your revision aids – books, notes, paper, computer – before you start and you will not be tempted to waste time.

- **R**emember to read your work back to yourself to make sure it makes sense and you have not made any silly mistakes.

- **E**very question on the paper will have a specified number of marks allocated. Check the marks that can be awarded. This will help you to know which questions are 'worth' more, and how much time you should spend on each answer.

- **E**nd each session of revision with a recap of the work you have done. If you read the notes over at the end of the session it will help you to remember.

> Actually, they weren't too bad!

- **N**ever give up! If you leave an answer to a question blank, you cannot get any marks. If you have a go you may at least pick up a few marks.

- And finally, remember to have an early night before the test. Last minute cramming does not work and you will be more relaxed if you are not exhausted.

There are two parts to this test: reading and writing.

Reading

The reading test you will take in Year 8 lasts 75 minutes with an extra 15 minutes reading time.

The reading answer booklet contains about 20 questions.

Some are easier than others, and this is reflected in the marks awarded.

The questions below are samples of the type of questions you will be asked on the paper. Try to answer them before looking at the sample answers.

They will help you to assess your progress.

The West Pier

Living and growing up in Brighton, I loved the sea, and spent many happy hours roaming the beaches; swimming, fishing, sailing on homemade rafts, baking potatoes on a driftwood fire. When the shingle beneath exploded like shrapnel, it only added to the pleasure. What else could a young boy want?

Us local kids bitterly resented the summer influx of thousands of daytrippers. 'London by the sea', they called our beloved town. The trippers used to swarm into Queen's Road from the trains, so many at times that they nearly stopped the trams. Past the Clock Tower, into West Street then onto the seafront. Like lemmings, the majority would turn left. Easily explainable; before them the panorama of countless pubs, cafés and ice cream parlours. On the lower promenade, all the joys of holiday-makers with their accompanying delicious odours. Stalls and shops selling bright rock in all shapes and sizes. Toothache by the yard. Candy floss, jellied eels, cockles and whelks, fish and chips smothered in onion vinegar – what ambrosia! More: silly hats of 'Kiss Me Quick' and many very saucy postcards. The jingling sound of little donkeys plodding along, sometimes bearing too heavy a load.

The cries of the boatmen, "Any more for the Skylark?" "Halfway to China for a bob!"

Then, dead ahead, the Palace pier, with Aladdin's caves stretching out below along the Upper Promenade.

The ghost train, hall of mirrors, and slot machines by the thousand. The trippers needed to go no further. The beaches around the Palace Pier and along to West Street were crowded with them. We locals used to turn right at the bottom of West Street, a parade of small shops, and the Palladium cinema, then the swish hotels: The Grand, The Metropole, and others. Over to the other side, even the Lower Promenade was more refined. Less shops and most of the small arches under the pavement were used as beach huts. Just before the war, a beautiful paddling pool was built. How that lovely strip of warm blue water used to attract us. Sadly, the age limit denied us the pleasure. The beaches were cleaner and less crowded and, above all, there was my goddess. Elegant and beautiful, gleaming in her pristine white paint, with eastern-type minarets on her brow, and the white foam of waves breaking around her feet, the West Pier – I fell in love.

Thinking back, I realise it wasn't only the architecture that attracted me; it was also possible to get to the first slot machine arcade without paying. When in funds, we would spend hours on the pier for a low admission price. Haunting the slot machines for the chance of a free go, annoying the fishermen at the southern end, and watching the rich go aboard the paddle steamer for a trip on the channel. We never got bored.

Then, in my thirteenth year, war was declared. It didn't seem to make a lot of difference to our lives, until suddenly the British Expeditionary Force was in full retreat and falling back on the French town of Dunkirk. Everything on Brighton beach that could float and a few that couldn't left to assist in the greatest seaborn rescue of any army that will ever be recorded. But worst of all for me, they blew a gaping great hole in my darling. The powers that be said that it was necessary to stop the German army using her as a landing stage if they invaded. Imagine a hole in the Pier holding up the seemingly invincible Wermacht for long! What nonsense! Us kids knew that all they needed to do was to leave the normal bloke in the ticket booth. If the Germans hadn't got the right money, they'd never have got by him! We'd tried for years and had failed.

Throughout the long years of the war, she stood lonely and neglected, white paint peeling and supports rusting. As I left England in 1945, the small troop ship I was on, instead of crossing direct to France, first of all steamed up the Channel past Brighton. One of my last glimpses of England was the West Pier.

In 1948, I returned and took a walk along the seafront to see what had become of her. From a distance, everything looked good. The hole had been repaired, the white paint glistened again. Closer inspection showed that further repair and routine maintenance were required.

As the years passed, her condition worsened. I was now married, and we were raising a family. I was in the fire brigade working a 24-hour-on, 24-hour-off shift system. I did a spare time job on my days off to raise more money. On my Sundays off I had plenty to do; no time for an old love.

I walked past her once with the family while the film *Oh What a Lovely War* was being made. We couldn't get on to the Pier, so we didn't stop. In 1970, the south end of the Pier was closed to the public followed by complete closure in 1975.

I often drove past her, noticing the further damage and neglect. When the hurricane struck, I thought it would be her end, but her strong heart and the genius of her designer and builder Eugenius Birch saw her through. Her condition worsened, and I, along with the majority of Brighton and Hove residents, was guilty of that neglect through indifference. Thank goodness some brave hearts fought on, and as a reward received some help from the National Lottery. A telephone number in the Argus brought me back into the picture. The paper ran an article saying that trips around the Pier were being arranged by the West Pier Trust. Anyone interested would, on the payment of fifteen pounds, be fitted with a hardhat and lifejacket and led around the Pier on a fixed route. I rang constantly – was the number always going to be engaged? But finally I got through. I will be meeting my old love again on 20th February at 3pm. I am in my seventieth year, and so excited I can hardly wait, feeling like that enchanted boy who first saw her in the 1930s. I hope she will forgive my neglect.

By Dave Huggins, *of Hove writer's group*

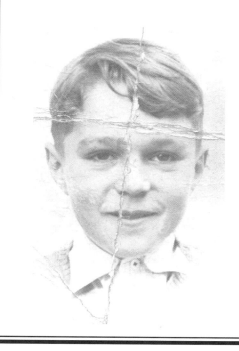

1 Read the second paragraph again. Find three examples of food with *delicious odours* mentioned by the author.

(1 mark)

2 Why do you think the author uses the simile *like lemmings* to describe the daytrippers?

(2 marks)

3 The author uses personification to make the West Pier into a beautiful woman. Choose and copy two quotations that show this.

(2 marks)

4 Why did the author have *no time for an old love?*

(1 mark)

5 How does the author use language to convey his sense of excitement at visiting the West Pier once more?

(3 marks)

Now read this extract:

Building the pier

The Pier was designed and engineered by Eugenius Birch to attract visitors and survive in the hostile environment of the seashore. It is a simple and functional structure built out from the sea using dozens of cast iron threaded columns screwed into the seabed and strengthened by a lattice of ties and girders that provide the necessary strength to support the promenade deck whilst allowing seas to pass harmlessly through.

Originally the West Pier had an open deck with only six small ornamental houses of oriental design, two toll houses and glass screens at the pier head to protect visitors from the wind and sun. In 1875 a central bandstand was added. In the 1880s weather screens the full length of the pier, steamer landing stages and a large pier head pavilion were constructed. The final building, completed in 1916, was a graceful concert hall. The result is seaside architecture at its finest, designed to attract and entertain holiday makers with all the pomp and frippery that is the essence of the English seaside resort. The pier is unique in being largely unaltered since that time, its proportions and style are unrivaled and its concert hall and theatre are two of the best surviving Victorian and Edwardian seaside entertainment buildings.

People and the pier

The West Pier story closely follows the changing fortunes of the English seaside holiday. It began simply as a promenade pier where visitors could enjoy the thrill of walking on water without the hazards of getting wet or being seasick. It was a place for the Victorian middle classes to socialise and exhibit their wealth, to see and be seen, to take in the sea air and admire the panoramic views of the land.

By the First World War it had evolved into a pleasure pier with a great variety of seaside entertainment both indoors and out. Throughout the twenties it was immensely popular, with attractions ranging from paddle steamer excursions, daring high divers and bathing from the pier head to military bands, recitals by the pier's resident orchestra in the concert hall and an all-year-round programme of plays, pantomimes and ballets in the theatre.

When the pier reopened after the Second World War it completed its evolution into a funfair pier. The theatre was converted into a restaurant on one floor and on the other the 'Laughter Land' games pavilion. The concert hall became a tea room, and the delights of the dodgems, helter-skelter, ghost train and miniature racing track could be enjoyed by all.

Britain's finest pier saved

Britain's finest pier has been saved from a watery grave by grants of approximately £14 million from the Heritage Lottery Fund.

Opened in 1866, the West Pier, Brighton, is the only Grade 1 Listed pier in the country. Derelict since 1975, it will undergo a three-year restoration. The remainder of the cost will be met by up to £30 million from private sector partners of the owners, the West Pier Trust.

The news ends a half century of decline for the structure which featured in the 1960s Richard Attenborough film Oh! What a Lovely War.

The Trust plan to restore the pier to the condition of its 1920s heyday. It is hoped that the sub-structure, decking and some kiosks will be complete in time for the celebration of New Year's Eve 1999. The full restoration should be complete by the Spring of year 2001.

While exact plans are not finalised, the redevelopment is likely to include upmarket restaurants, bars, entertainment and possibly hotel accommodation. There will be full public access for strolling, shopping and fishing.

Oliver Peyton of Gruppo, one of the Trust's private sector partners, commented: "We're very proud to be involved in the redevelopment of the West Pier. Our plan is *to create a unique, all-year-round and internationally-acclaimed destination resort on the English coast."*

Dr Geoff Lockwood, Chief Executive of the West Pier Trust said: "Brighton has had a unique buzz since Regency days. A racy, fashionable, metropolitan, theatrical and architecturally innovative image blending with the mass popular appeal of the seafront from the day-tripper railway age. The restoration of the West Pier and the high-style activities it will host will add 21st century fizz to the traditional Brighton buzz.

"The Brighton seafront is twin-engined. It has had to fly on one engine for far too long. Now it will regain balance and pick up speed for the 21st century.

"The real work starts now. We have not climbed Everest, but have secured the finance necessary for the climb."

Brighton & Hove Council Leader, Lord Bassam added: "This is a momentous announcement. It is hard to convey the excitement this award will create locally in Brighton, Hove and Sussex.

"In recent years our historic seafront has been transformed with big investments of public and private money, but a renovated West Pier will be the crowning glory.

"As an internationally famous building, it will also signal Brighton and Hove's renaissance to the rest of the world."

Chair of the council's Arts, Recreation and Tourism Committee Councillor Ian Duncan said: "Its impact on local tourism should be significant, providing a boost for hotels, shops, restaurants and other attractions."

6 How did Eugenius Birch design the Pier to withstand the force of the sea?

(3 marks)

7 Read the section headed *People and the Pier*.

Draw three lines to match each paragraph to a topic.

Draw only one line to each box.

    A: Post war developments   paragraph one

    B: The Victorian middle class on holiday   paragraph two

    C: Between the wars   paragraph three

                                                            (1 mark)

8 The article aims to tell people about the history of the Pier, making it sound as though it is important to restore it. How successful is the article?

You should write about:

• how language is used to make the Pier seem historically important

• how the writer uses language to make the Pier sound attractive.

                                                      (5 marks)

TEST PAPER 2

Writing

The tasks in the Year 8 writing test are to *explore*, *imagine*, *entertain*, and to *analyse*, *review*, *comment*.

The test you take at school will last 75 minutes.

There are two writing tasks. The major task is a longer piece which is more open-ended, giving you a chance to write in your own style. The minor task is more specific, and asks you to write more briefly and to the point to answer the question.

You will be given planning sheets to help you to organise your work.

The test will assess your ability to:
- write imaginatively
- organise your ideas and present them effectively
- use paragraphs in a logical way
- vary sentences to create effects
- use punctuation correctly
- choose interesting, varied and appropriate vocabulary.

Major task (You should spend about 50 minutes on this question.)

Imagine you are returning to a place you loved as a child with your own grandchildren. You are sad to notice the way in which the resort has changed – but your grandchildren in their turn think the resort is wonderful.

(Use the planning sheet overleaf to help.)

(30 marks)

Planning

Before you start your writing, make some brief notes to help you to organise your ideas.

Place_____

_____

_____

What it was like when you were a child/attractions for children and teenagers:

_____

_____

How do you think the resort has deteriorated?

_____

_____

What do your grandchildren like?

_____

_____

Has the resort changed, or is it you?

_____

_____

_____

Useful vocabulary:

_____

_____

_____

Minor task (You should spend about 25 minutes on this question.)

Think of a place you have been on a day trip. This could be a theme park, a museum or a gallery. It should be somewhere you would recommend to others.

Write a review of the place for a student magazine.

You should write briefly, reviewing the facilities available.

Write a conclusion, saying why you think the venue is a good place to visit.

(20 marks)

Before you start writing, make some brief notes to organise your ideas.

Name of the place:_____

_____

_____

_____

What is there?

_____

_____

_____

What general facilities are available?

_____

_____

_____

Why recommend it?

_____

_____

_____

ANSWERS

Answers to exercises

Apostrophes
Exercise 1

1 The tiger's tail swished angrily. She ate her pieces of meat warily, her eyes flicking at every movement. The boy tried not to move, but the insects were biting. Sunil's leg twitched suddenly, and the tiger's eyes found him there.

2 The dog's breath was rancid. The girl's nose wrinkled in her sleep, then one eye wearily opened. The girl's eyes popped open in surprise as she saw the large shaggy creature bending over her. "Bramble!" she cried. "What are you doing in here? Fetch my slippers, girl!" As she sat up, Beth wondered where the other dogs were.

3 The singer's voice was low and mellow, but her eyes were glittering with excitement.

4 The old woman's bags were heavy and it was a long way to the bus stop.

5 The magician's wand seemed to have a life of its own. The wand's tip sparked and flamed wildly until the performer's hat was set alight.

Exercise 2

1 There wasn't time to go to the shops, so I didn't get any milk.

2 The band wasn't very good. I've seen better.

3 We're not going to the pictures tonight because we've seen the film already.

4 They're not coming to see us, so it doesn't matter if you can't come.

Exercise 3

"It is funny," Bethany said to Sarah. "I do not usually like sporty types, but there is something about him that is attractive."

"I would not mind a date with him either!" said Sarah.

"Come on," Bethany sighed. "We have got double maths next, and old Clarkie will go nuts if we are late! And he will not accept 'Sorry, we were busy eyeing boys' as an excuse!"

Prefixes and suffixes
Exercise 1

1 intergalactic – *inter* means *between* and *galactic* means to do with *galaxies*

2 disproportionate – not in proportion

3 extinguish – put out, as in a candle

4 monosyllabic – speaking in words of one syllable

5 tripartite – a three-part system

6 biography – someone's life story

7 intermediate – in between/in the middle

8 meaningless – to have no meaning

Exercise 2

The students were <u>dis</u>interest<u>ed</u> in the lecture because the teacher spoke in a <u>mono</u>logue. Her voice was bor<u>ing</u>, but also <u>in</u>audible. She was completely hope<u>less</u>, and Rosie <u>auto</u>matic<u>ally</u> slump<u>ed</u> back in her seat as the lecture began. <u>Dis</u>interest<u>ed</u> students fidget<u>ed</u>, sharpen<u>ed</u> pencils and star<u>ed</u> out of windows as the lectur<u>er</u> began to read from her own biography.

Ideas and opinions
Exercise 1

We know Lindsey feels depressed because the writer says she *slumped* onto the bench, *ignoring* her cat because she is in a bad mood. The author says she feels *terrible*. Her mood changes when James appears. The author says, *Her face was flushed, and her eyes shone brightly.* This is because she is very pleased to see James.

Exercise 2

The newts swam away when they saw the girl's shadow. They watched her from behind the plants. Vicky was fascinated by newts – she thought they looked like aliens. She remembered collecting newts as a child for a project, and how they'd been rehomed in the school pond. The children had needed permission to touch the newts as they are a protected species.

Speech marks
Exercise 1

1 My mum said that she didn't want to go to Birmingham, but I jumped up and said "I do!"

2 "Good grief!" said Helen. "I'd hate it if I had to live here!"

3 Sheila said that she liked living in Brighton because it was at the seaside.

4 "It's Hove, actually," Dave complained.

5 "I like going on the Pier best," drooled Bethany, "because I love the hot doughnut stalls."

6 Alex argued with his sister. He said that he preferred the rock shops under the promenade.

7 "Well, I like playing on the beach best!" shrieked Eleanor, as she splashed the water at them both.

Exercise 2

Alexander asked his mum what the time was. He said that he was meeting Simon at six. His mother asked if he needed his dinner first, but that it was not ready. Alexander told her he would reheat it when he got home and that he wouldn't be late. His mother asked him where he was going. He told her he was going nowhere special. Then his mother asked if he was going with or without his entourage. Alexander laughed that he didn't know what she meant. His mother told him she meant the adoring girls who normally followed him around. Then Alexander shrugged and told her he would see her later.

Special vocabulary

Exercise 1
1 W84ME – wait for me
2 YRUL8 – why are you late?
3 URGR8 – you are great
4 RUOK – are you OK?
5 OIC – Oh, I see
6 BCNU – be seeing you
7 T2UL – talk to you later
8 NO1M8 – number one mate

Exercise 2
1 CUL8R
2 T4U
3 W84ME
4 URL8
5 URAGR8M8
6 IC
7 BCNU
8 THNQ

Formal and informal writing

Exercise 2
require – formal; want – informal; okay – informal; adequate – formal; as soon as you can; at your earliest convenience – formal; won't – informal; will not – formal; excellent – formal; great – informal; inform – formal; tell – informal; ask – informal; enquire – formal;

Yours sincerely – formal; See you later – informal; suggest – formal; tell – informal

Standard and dialectal language

Exercise 2
puddock – frog
lochan – lake
thocht – thought
hurdies – haunches; top of his legs
cockit – cocked; put on one side
heid – head
throu' – through
seggs – sedge grass

Exercise 3
Ye knaa what ah mean leik.
Do you know what I mean?
How man mutha man.
Please, mother, don't embarrass me.
Eeeh man, ahm gannin te the booza.
Okay, I have had enough, I am going to the bar.
Hoy yer hamma ower heor hinny.
Pass me the hammer darling.
Whees i' the netty?
Who's in the lavatory?
Gan canny or we'll dunsh summick.
Be careful or we will crash into something.

Modern and old English

Exercise 1
1 wench – girl
2 hath – has
3 gallant – handsome young man
4 stain'd With grief – sad; had been crying
5 beauty's canker – the bad or rotten thing about beauty
6 might'st – might

Structuring sentences

Exercise 1
The first two sentences are short, and this sounds like Isobel is stopping and starting as though afraid. As the sentences lengthen, it sounds as though Isobel is getting braver and moving further into the room. The complex sentences at the end of the passage completely change the mood; Isobel is now curious.

Organising work

Exercise 1
I think the author started a new paragraph to talk about the mist because it was a different thing than the rubbish and pollution he had

been describing in the first paragraph. The third paragraph ... introduces another new thing – the town of the dead. The new paragraph used gives the idea of the town of the dead impact.

Exercise 2

David hoped it wasn't one of the mangy pups that loitered around the store for the scraps thrown by Old Johnny as he cleared out at the end of the day.

THIS NEW PARAGRAPH NEEDED BECAUSE OF THE SUDDEN CHANGE OF MOOD

Suddenly, a clown appeared, bursting out of the circle with a blood-chilling yell. But it wasn't a clown. It was Win. And his beautiful chestnut skin, the colour of burnished copper, was clogged with the contents of his Ma's provisions bag.

THIS NEW PARAGRAPH SHOWS THAT SOMEONE NEW IS SPEAKING.

"Now you're the right colour to shop in Old Johnny's!" laughed a tall boy with unfeasibly short hair. It wasn't a pleasant laugh.

Review your own work

Exercise 1

Some suggested answers.

1 I adore chocolate cake more than any other cake in the world. A good chocolate cake should be moist and fragrant, crumbling easily as you bite it. My favourite icing is chewy fudge frosting.

2 I play in a band called *Spraydog*, rehearsing at weekends and sometimes in the evenings. We often play at gigs organised by the community centre. We play mainly indie-pop but stray into rock sometimes.

3 My favourite animal is my big, black cat.

4 My school plays lots of team games, including netball, rounders, football, hockey and basketball. My favourite is football because I am very good at it.

Exercise 2

Mewlius Caesar was the leader of the colony of feral cats. He wasn't as fierce or big as some of the other cat, but he was a leader nevertheless.

He was white with black patches that made him look as though he had knocked a pot of white paint on his back.

He loved to lie in the sun but still never missed the opportunity to snuggle up to his human family.

He was a grand old man and we still miss him.

Writing for an audience

Exercise 3

An older, possibly adult audience, due to the subject matter – which seems a little dark, and threatening – and the vocabulary, such as *plasma*.

General spelling rules

Exercise 1

1 The weather was <u>changeable</u> (changeable). As <u>allways</u> (always), the <u>ladys</u> (ladies) were collecting the fruit from the <u>feild</u> (field).

2 The <u>ladys</u> (ladies) <u>admited</u> (admitted) that the marks on the <u>cieling</u> (ceiling) were the result of their football game.

3 The hotel <u>submited</u> (submitted) a bill for the damage, which was quite <u>noticable</u> (noticeable) as the room was entered.

4 <u>Untill</u> (until) the bill was <u>setled</u> (settled), the <u>ladys</u> (ladies) were not allowed to go home.

Figurative language

Exercise 1

1 The sun was an orange, thrown into the sky by a playful child. (M – the writer says the sun was an orange.

2 The cat snored with a noise like the rumble of distant thunder, muffled by cloud. (S)

3 The dragonfly was a crystal Spitfire, swooping over the heads of the bobbing sedge grass. (M)

4 The car was as sluggish as an elderly camel, limping up the hill. (S)

5 The wrinkles on her face were a road map, showing all the journeys, joyful and unhappy, that she had made. (M)

6 The sky was as blue as a blackbird's egg. (S)

7 The baby's ear was a tiny perfect shell. (M)

A personal word bank

Exercise 1

Some suggested answers.

1 walk – slouched, crept, slithered, wandered

2 small – tiny, minuscule, microscopic, miniature

3 big – enormous, gigantic, enormous, huge, great

4 run – gallop, sprint, lollop

5 sad – miserable, low, depressed

6 happy – cheery, merry, joyous

7 make – form, create, design

8 go – travel, move, visit

9 nice – lovely, pretty, sweet

10 funny – amusing, hilarious, entertaining

Reading between the lines

Exercise 1

Some suggestions.

The poem calls Billy a champion because he has a strong spirit. He obviously does not have an easy life – he has holes in his jersey, and he has to win at marbles to afford to eat. We know he has had no breakfast because the poem says *he'd sell his winnings/And buy breakfast at lunchtime.*

Exercise 2

Some suggestions.

Grace Nichols is explaining how homesick she feels, describing all the things she misses.

Grammar

Exercise 1

Some suggested answers.

1 The firefighter put on his protective hat because it was hot.
The fire was hot, so the firefighter put on his protective hat.

2 The woman stroked the cat because she was beautiful.
The cat was beautiful so the woman stroked her.

3 The boy hugged the dog because he was afraid.
The boy was afraid so he hugged the dog or
The dog was afraid so the boy hugged him.

4 The crab ate the whole fish, because it was huge.
The crab was huge so it ate the whole fish.

5 If that baby doesn't want its milk, throw it away.

Throw the milk away if the baby doesn't want it.

6 The leak was repaired before any damage was done by the woman.
The woman repaired the leak before any damage was done.

Exercise 2

1 The dog ate the meat because it was brown.

2 The girl liked the horse because she was beautiful.

3 The boy cut his finger on the knife because it was sharp.

4 The mouse ate the smelly cheese as it was smelly.

5 The bat flew into the window because it was transparent.

6 The elephant squirted the tree with water because it was green and slimy.

Answers to Test Paper 1

1 Any of the following: candy floss, jellied eels, cockles and whelks, fish and chips smothered in onion vinegar, rock.

2 'The author uses the word *lemmings* because there are a lot of holiday makers.'
(This answer would be worth 1 mark as it partially answers the question.)

'The author compares the daytrippers to *lemmings* because they all seem to go in the same direction. He says that they *swarm*, and that word is usually used to describe insects or animals. It creates the sense that the daytrippers have no individual will, but just follow each other.'
(This answer would be worth 2 marks as it refers directly to the words used, quoting from the text to support the answer given.)

3 Any two of these quotations:
• *My goddess. Elegant and beautiful, gleaming in her pristine white paint, with eastern-type minarets on her brow, and the white foam of waves breaking around her feet, the West Pier.*
• *... my darling.*
• *I returned and took a walk along the seafront to see what had become of her.*
• *... her condition worsened.*
• *I walked past her once...*
• *I often drove past her...*

- *I thought it would be her end, but her strong heart and the genius of her designer and builder Eugenius Birch saw her through. Her condition worsened ...*
- *I will be meeting my old love again ...*
- *... feeling like that enchanted boy who first saw her in the 1930s. I hope she will forgive my neglect.*

4 'He had a family.'
(This answer would not get the mark because it misses out part of the answer.)
'The author had a family, and was working a busy shift pattern in the fire brigade. He also had a part time job for his days off, so he had no time to go to the pier.'
(This answer would get full marks as it contains all of the reasons why the author had no spare time.)

5 *I rang constantly – was the number always going to be engaged? But finally I got through. I will be meeting my old love again on 20th February at 3pm. I am in my seventieth year, and so excited I can hardly wait, feeling like that enchanted boy who first saw her in the 1930s. I hope she will forgive my neglect.*
'The author uses short sentences, as though he is breathless with excitement. The words he uses such as *hardly wait*, help to convey his impatience to see the Pier again.'
(This answer would earn full marks because it supports ideas with a carefully chosen quotation, and comments on the sentence structure used by the author to build mood.)

6 'Eugenius Birch made the Pier strong enough to stand against the battering of the sea by using *dozens of cast iron threaded columns screwed into the seabed and strengthened by a lattice of ties and girders that provide the necessary strength to support the promenade deck whilst allowing seas to pass harmlessly through.* This means that the legs of the pier were embedded into the seabed, and these were reinforced by a network of iron girders. The network of metal was stronger than a solid structure would have been,

because it offered less resistance to the force of the waves, which passed through the legs of the pier instead of pushing against them.'
(Full marks for answering the question fully, using a carefully chosen quotation to support the answer. The quotation was in turn explained, and this made the answer very clear.)

7 A3, B1, C2

8 'The final building, completed in 1916, was a graceful concert hall. The result is seaside architecture at its finest, designed to attract and entertain holidaymakers with all the pomp and frippery that is the essence of the English seaside resort. The pier is unique in being largely unaltered since that time, its proportions and style are unrivalled and its concert hall and theatre are two of the best surviving Victorian and Edwardian seaside entertainment buildings.'
The writer uses words such as *graceful* to describe the Pier; this makes it sound attractive. The writer also says that the Pier is described as *seaside architecture at its finest*, which makes it sound like a very good example of a Pier. The writer tells the audience that the Pier is *unique in being largely unaltered* since the time it was built in 1916. The Pier is also described as having a concert hall and theatre that are *two of the best surviving Victorian and Edwardian seaside entertainment buildings.* It is the sense that the pier is *one of a kind* that makes it historically important, and worthy of conservation.'
(This is a good answer because it addresses the points in the question, and uses quotations to support the answers given.)

Ambiguity

when meaning is unclear

Apostrophe

a punctuation mark used to show possession (*Eleanor's bunny*) or contraction (*don't, haven't*)

Ascender

the 'stick' on a letter such as *d* or *b*

Cliché

an overused phrase such as *It's raining cats and dogs*

Complex sentence

complex sentences contain several ideas, often separated by commas

Compound sentence

a compound sentence links two or more simple sentences using conjunctions, such as *because*

Consonant

the letters of the alphabet except the vowels

Contraction

a shortened word or abbreviation, such as *doesn't, can't, won't*

Descender

the 'tails' on letters such as g and y

Dialect

locally-occurring words and phrases used in informal speech

Genre

different types of writing such as science fiction, romance, horror

Imagery

descriptive writing uses imagery such as similes and metaphors to make interesting 'word pictures'

Lower case

those letters which are not capitals

Metaphor

a metaphor describes something as though it were something else: *The raindrops were glassy pebbles, thrown by a giant's hand*

Personification

a special type of metaphor which describes an inanimate (non living) object as a person: *Winter is a white-haired old man.*

Précis

a piece of writing is a shortened version that just covers the most important points

Prefix

a syllable with a meaning of its own that occurs at the beginning of a word such as *pre-* and *bi-*

Simile

a type of description that says something is like something else: *The cat's tail uncoiled like a stripy jungle snake.*

Simple sentence

a simple sentence has just one idea.

Suffix

a syllable with a meaning of its own that occurs at the end of a word such as *-less* or *-able*

Syllable

a unit of sound made up of letters. *Cat* has one syllable; *football* has two

Upper case

capital letters

Vowel

the letters a, e, i, o and u

INDEX